W9-DDZ-977

HIDDEN HONOLULU

From the Good Life
To the Great Outdoors

Other travel books from And/Or Press:

Hidden Hawaii: The Adventurer's Guide by Ray Riegert. This invaluable resource covers everything the island traveler needs — from budget hotels to home-made restaurants to hidden beaches.

Along the Gringo Trail by Jack Epstein. This indispensible guide to budget and adventure travel in Latin America goes far beyond the usual guidebook information on transportation, hotels, and restaurants.

The Art and Adventure of Traveling Cheaply by Rick Berg. A veteran traveler reveals inside tips on extended budget adventures throughout the world.

Mountain Wilderness Survival by Craig Patterson. Enjoy the rigors and beauty of our wilderness areas armed with the information in this straight-forward, versatile, and humorous manual.

Vagabonding in the U.S.A. by Ed Buryn. Discover a new America with this exuberant guide to the joys and realities of vagabonding.

HIDDEN

HONOLULU

From the Good Life . . .

to the Great Outdoors

by Ray Riegert

And/Or Press
Berkeley · California

Published and distributed by: And/Or Press, Inc.
P.O. Box 2246
Berkeley, CA 94702

Library of Congress Cataloging in Publication Data
Riegert, Ray, 1947
Hidden Honolulu.

Bibliography: p. 161
Includes index.
1. Honolulu (Hawaii)—Description—Guide-books.
I. Title.
DU629.H7R53 919.69'31044 82-1608

ISBN 0-915904-63-2 AACR2

Printed in the U.S.A. by BookCrafters

First Printing: April 1982

10 9 8 7 6 5 4 3 2 1 (current printing)

Project Coordinator: Carlene Schnabel
Book Design & Art Direction: Carlene Schnabel
Illustration: Jen-Ann Kirchmeier
Editing & Indexing: Sayre Van Young
Research Assistance: Leslie Henriques
Cover Photography: Allan Seiden, Werner Stoy
Cover Typography: Solotype
Maps: Marlyn Amann, Alison McDonald

Book Production by BookPack, Inc.:

Production Director: Ray Riegert

Typesetters:
Kay Murray-Nears
Allen Hayward
Diane Valay

Layout & Paste-up Artists:
Tim Lewis
Beee Langley
Phil Gardner

Proofreaders:
Leslie Henriques
Kris Johnson

Consultant: Sam Lawson

For my sisters — Claudia, Deb, Jan, and Pat — and my brother Rusty, who have always been to me more than any brother could ask.

Acknowledgements

The author's credit on the cover of a book is often misleading. Glancing at that solitary byline beneath the title, one might assume that a single person was responsible. Actually, most books require the energy of several people whose pleading and prompting help carry the author.

This particular volume owes much to Bruce LoPucki, who encouraged me from the project's very inception. Sebastian Orfali and Carlene Schnabel demonstrated that rare combination of faith, patience, and enthusiasm required of talented publishers. Sayre Van Young contributed her outstanding editing abilities. In Honolulu, Lindy Boyes of the Hawaii Visitors Bureau assisted with my travel itinerary, while on the mainland Linda Lyons gave advice. I also want to thank all the folks from And/Or Press, BookPack, and I.N.K., Inc. who worked on the project.

Now that I've added a few footnotes to that byline, I should note that there is one person who can never be credited sufficiently. Not only has she donated ideas, editing skills, and research time, she has also endured the tantrums and traumas of a writer on deadline. I want to especially thank my wife Leslie.

Nothing had prepared me for Honolulu... So strange and so charming associations are attached to the name, that at first I could hardly believe my eyes.... It is the meeting-place of East and West. The very new rubs shoulders with the immeasurably old. And if you have not found the romance you expected you have come upon something singularly intriguing.

W. Somerset Maugham, 1921

Contents

HIDDEN HONOLULU

Introduction

Honolulu, as Somerset Maugham remarks, is the place where East encounters West. Nowhere in the world will you find a population more varied or an ambience as striking. A sultry city of 600,000, it is America's authentic melting pot, spiced with a dozen cultures.

This is a region of sharp contrast and wild color. One day you'll scan a sun-dappled city backdropped by billowy clouds and razor peaks; the next it will appear as a high-rise metropolis with a thriving commercial center and booming waterfront, home port for financial tycoons and sea weary sailors alike.

Today this luxurious city by the sea serves as the hub of Hawaii, determining the cultural, economic, and political life of the islands. Its burgeoning commerce and strategic location have made Honolulu the capital not only of our fiftieth state, but of the Pacific as well. The deepwater port here draws cargo ships from across the ocean, while the unmatched tropical climate attracts touring visitors from around the globe.

Honolulu's lure for travelers can be found also in crystal blue waters and white-sand beaches, bronzed beach boys and luscious Polynesian women, and in those volcanic mountains rising in the hazy distance. Life in this island city is both relaxing and rejuvenating; the possibilities it provides are unparalleled.

As you disembark from the plane and begin exploring Honolulu, a multifarious environment opens to view.

Traveling east from the city's international airport toward Waikiki, you'll skim the waterfront. The tankers and freighters anchored here fly the flags of every nation imaginable. That forest of skyscrapers in whose shadow they stand is the downtown Honolulu financial district, with its international corporations and historic old buildings. A world away, and several blocks down the street, is the city's Chinatown, a tumbledown collection of clapboard buildings and mom 'n' pop stores. Not far from this Asian enclave sits Punchbowl, the gently rounded crater of an ancient volcano. A ridge of sharp-backed mountains protects the entire city. These are the Koolaus, in one of whose valleys nestles the beautiful University of Hawaii campus.

Spreading carpet-like beneath the familiar silhouette of Diamond Head, lies the city's most famous district. If Honolulu is the heart of the Pacific, Waikiki is its pulse. Less than one square mile in area, it packs more fun and glamor per punch than anyplace in the world. There are times when Waikiki's Parisian-size boulevards seem ready to explode from the sheer force of the crowds. People in bikinis and exotic *aloha* shirts stroll the streets, while others flash past on mopeds or in rickshaws. The beach, a sparkling swath of pearly sand that stretches endlessly, has drawn sun-worshippers and water lovers since the days of Hawaiian royalty. In ancient times Waikiki Beach was a retreat for Hawaiian kings; today it's a spectacular strip lined with gourmet restaurants and first-class hotels.

If your tastes parallel those of most Hawaii visitors, you'll be spending significant time in this vibrant spot. So I have tried to provide ample information on Waikiki's outstanding facilities, while also detailing the rest of Honolulu. Chapter I should help familiarize you with the customs and history of Hawaii. The second chapter will aid in planning your trip and making plane reservations. Chapter III is dedicated to the Honolulu "good life," and describes the city's marvelous conveniences. Here you'll find current information on car rentals, hotels, restaurants, shopping, and nightlife throughout Waikiki and greater Honolulu; all these listings are arranged by purse size, ranging from budget to ultra-deluxe. Be you a budgeter or a big spender, you should have no problem finding the right accommodations. Chapter IV carries you into the "great outdoors," describing the sights and sports available to Honolulu visitors. Here you'll encounter everything from air-conditioned bus tours to surfing safaris. The fifth chapter explores Oahu, the island of which Honolulu is part; you'll find what to expect when venturing out on daytrips from town. Chapter VI briefly sketches the other islands in the Hawaiian chain, in case you want to add an extra adventure to your Honolulu sojourn.

The rest is up to you. With its sun-spangled days and scintillating nights, Honolulu is the modern world's answer to paradise. It's a city that offers practically everything; all you need do is decide what you'd like, then go out and discover it. The purpose of this book is to help you do just that. *Aloha* and have fun.

CHAPTER I

Capital of Paradise

Honolulu Today

THE LAND

The pearl of the Pacific is a city set 2,500 miles southwest of Los Angeles, on the same 20th latitude as Hong Kong and Mexico City. Among its many other facets, this sparkling metropolis serves as the capital of our fiftieth state. Unique among government centers however, Honolulu oversees a state which comprises 132 islands stretching for more than 1,500 miles across the North Pacific.

At the southeastern end of this chain are the six major islands (including Oahu, where Honolulu is situated) which we know as Hawaii. If Oahu were placed alongside the others (Maui, Hawaii, Kauai, Molokai, and Lanai), and those hundred-odd islets were included as well, the total land area would be equal only to that of Connecticut and Rhode Island. Honolulu, it seems, is the capital of the longest, skinniest, most disjointed state in the Union.

There are several other points to remember about this unique city. First of all, it's two hours earlier in the "Big Papaya" than in Los Angeles, four hours before Chicago, and five hours earlier than New York. Since Hawaii does not observe daylight savings, this time difference becomes one hour greater during summer months.

Another thing to keep in mind is that Honolulu's home island of Oahu, like other islands in the archipelago, is practically a small continent. Volcanic mountains rise in the interior while the coastline is fringed with coral reefs and white-sand beaches. The northeastern face of the island, buffeted by trade winds, is the wet side. The contrast between this region and the southern sector around Honolulu is sometimes startling. Rain clouds may be massing along the island's rustic North Shore, while cosmopolitan Honolulu is enjoying brilliant beach weather. For the visitor, this means you can luxuriate in the city, then head out to the country to experience several diverse environments.

THE PEOPLE

Because of its unique history and isolated geography, Honolulu is truly a cultural melting pot. It's the capital of the only state in the union in which white people are a minority group. Whites, or *haoles* as they're called in the islands, comprise only about twenty-nine percent of Hawaii's 900,000 population. Japanese constitute twenty-eight percent, Hawaiians and part-Hawaiians account for eighteen percent, Filipinos ten percent, Chinese about five percent, and other racial groups ten percent.

Five out of every six residents live on the island of Oahu, and most of those live in the city of Honolulu. It's a very young, vital society. Almost half the community is under twenty-five, and over one-quarter of the people were born of racially mixed parents.

One trait characterizing many of these people is Hawaii's famous spirit of *aloha*, a genuine friendliness, an openness to strangers, a willingness to give freely. Undoubtedly, it is one of the finest qualities any people has ever demonstrated. *Aloha* originated with the Polynesians and played an important role in ancient Hawaiian civilization. And today you'll find it as prevalent in Honolulu as anywhere in this enchanting island chain.

THE ECONOMY

For years sugar was king in Hawaii, the most lucrative part of the island economy. Today tourism is number one. Two-and-a-half million Americans, and almost four million travelers worldwide, visit Honolulu every year. It's now a two-billion-dollar business that expanded logarithmically during the 1960s and 1970s.

With 125,000 personnel and dependents stationed in Hawaii, the U.S. military is the second-largest industry. Concentrated on Oahu, the armed forces pour about one billion dollars into the local economy every year.

Among Hawaii's official cash crops, sugar is still tops. While the $366 million sugar industry is small potatoes compared to tourism and the military, Hawaii remains America's largest sugar-producing state. But sugar, like everything else in the islands, is threatened by urban development. A ton of water is required to produce a pound of sugar. Since the construction industry is now practically a one-billion-dollar-a-year business, new housing developments are competing more and more with sugar cane for the precious liquid.

Pineapple is another crop that's ailing. Stiff competition from the Philippines has reduced Hawaii's pineapple plantations to six.

Hawaii is still the only place in the United States that grows coffee. The islands do a booming business in macadamia nuts, orchids, anthuriums, guava nectar, and passion fruit juice. Together these industries have created a strong economy in the fiftieth state. The per capita income is greater than the national average, and the standard of living is generally higher.

Important note: Honolulu possesses one of the highest costs of living in the United States. As in the rest of the country, inflation is no stranger here; price increases are common. Therefore, don't be surprised if the prices quoted in this book are sometimes lower than those you'll actually be paying.

THE CUISINE

Nowhere is the influence of Hawaii's chop suey population stronger than in the kitchen. While in Honolulu, you'll probably eat not only with a fork, but with chopsticks and fingers as well. You'll sample a wonderfully varied cuisine. In addition to standard American fare, dozens of restaurants serve Hawaiian, Japanese, Chinese, Korean, Portuguese, and Filipino dishes. There are also fresh fruits aplenty — plus native fish such as *mahimahi*, marlin, and snapper.

The prime Hawaiian dish is *poi*, made from crushed taro root and served as a pasty purple liquid. It's pretty bland fare, but it does make a good side dish with roast pork or tripe stew. You should also try *lau lau*, a combination of fish, pork, and taro leaves wrapped in a *ti* leaf and steamed. And don't neglect to taste baked *ulu* (breadfruit) and *opihi* (limpets). A good way to try all these dishes at one sitting is to attend a *luau*. You might watch the newpapers for one of the special *luaus* sponsored by civic organizations; or better yet, check the listings contained herein for *luaus* sponsored by hotels and private companies in Honolulu.

Japanese dishes include sukiyaki, teriyaki, and tempura, plus an island favorite—*sashimi,* or raw fish. Similarly, Chinese menus usually feature the dishes you've sampled at home as well as some less common treats. Among these are *saimin*, a noodle soup filled with meat and vegetables, and crack seed, a delicacy made from dried fruits.

You can count on the Koreans for *kim chi,* a spicy salad of pickled cabbage, and *kun koki*, barbecued meat prepared with soy and sesame oil. The Portuguese serve up some delicious sweets including *malasadas* (donuts minus the holes) and *pao doce*, or sweet bread. For Filipino fare, I recommend *adobo*, a pork or chicken dish spiced with garlic and vinegar, and *pochero*, a meat entree cooked with bananas and several vegetables.

As the Hawaiians say, *"Hele mai ai."* Come and eat!

THE LANGUAGE

The language common to all Hawaii is English, but because of its diverse cultural heritage, the archipelago also supports several other tongues. Foremost among these are Hawaiian and pidgin.

Hawaiian, closely related to other Polynesian languages, is one of the most fluid and melodious languages in the world. It's composed of only twelve letters: five vowels—*a, e, i, o, u* and seven consonants—*h, k, l, m, n, p, w*.

At first glance, the language appears formidable: how the heck do you pronounce *humuhumunukunukuapuaa*? But actually it's all quite simple. After you've mastered a few rules of pronunciation, you can take on any word in the language.

The first thing to remember is that every syllable ends with a vowel, and the next to last syllable receives the accent.

The next rule to keep in mind is that all the letters in Hawaiian are pronounced. Consonants are pronounced the same as in English (except for the *w*, which is pronounced as a *v* when it introduces the last syllable of a word—as in *ewa* or *awa*). Vowels are pronounced the same as in Latin or Spanish: *a* as in *among*, *e* as in *they*, *i* as in *machine*, *o* as in *no*, and *u* as in *too*. Hawaiian has four vowel combinations or diphthongs: *au* pronounced *ow*, *ae* and *ai*, which sound like *eye*, and *ei*, pronounced *ay*.

An important fact to remember when visiting Honolulu is that directions are rarely given in terms of "east" and "west." The Hawaiian way is to direct people with reference to landmarks: east is *diamondhead*, or in the direction of the fabled crater; west is *ewa*, toward the old plantation town of Ewa; north translates as *mauka*, toward the mountains; and south is *makai*, toward the sea.

By now you're probably wondering what I could possibly have meant when I said Hawaiian was simple. I think the glossary which follows will simplify everything while helping you pronounce common words and place names. Just go through the list, starting with words like *aloha* and *luau* that you already know. After you've practiced pronouncing familiar words, the rules will become second nature; you'll practically be a *kamaaina*.

Just when you start to speak with a swagger, cocky about having learned a new language, some young Hawaiian will start talking at you in a tongue that breaks all the rules you've so carefully mastered. That's pidgin. It started in the nineteenth century as a lingua franca among Hawaii's many races. Pidgin speakers mix English and Hawaiian with several other tongues to produce a spicy creole. It's a fascinating language with its own vocabulary, a unique syntax, and a rising inflection that's hard to mimic.

Pidgin is definitely the in way to talk in Hawaii. A lot of young Hawaiians use it among themselves as a private language. At times they may start talking pidgin to you, acting as though they don't speak English; then if they decide you're okay, they'll break into English. When that happens, you be one *da kine brah*.

So *brah*, I take *da kine* pidgin words, put 'em together with Hawaiian, make one big list. Savvy?

HAWAIIAN VOCABULARY

aa (**ah**-ah) - a type of rough lava
ae (eye) - yes
aikane (eye-**kah**-nay) - friend
akamai (ah-**kah**-my) - wise
alii (ah-**lee**-ee) - chief
aloha (ah-**lo**-ha) - hello; greetings; love
*aole (ah-***oh**-lay) - no
auwe (ow-**way**) - ouch!
brah (bra) - friend; brother
bumby (**bum**-bee) - after awhile; by and by
dah makule guys (da mah-**kuh**-lay guys) - senior citizens
da kine (da kyne) - whatdyacallit; thingamajig; that way
duh uddah time (duh **uh**-duh time) - once before
diamondhead - in an easterly direction
ewa (**eh**-vah) - in a westerly direction
hale (**hah**-lay) - house
haole (**how**-lee) - Caucasian; white person
hapa (**hah**-pa) - half
hapa-haole (**hah**-pa **how**-lee) - half-Caucasian
heiau (hey-ee-**ow**) - temple
hele on (**hey**-lay own) - hip; with it
holo holo (**ho**-low **ho**-low) - to visit
howzit? (hows-it) - how you doing? what's happening?
hukilau (**who**-key-lau) - community fishing party
hula (**who**-la) - Hawaiian dance
imu (**ee**-moo) - underground oven
ipo (**ee**-po) - sweetheart
jag up (jag up) - drunk
kahuna (kah-**who**-nah) - priest
kai (kye) - ocean
kamaaina (kah-mah-**eye**-nah) - longtime island resident
kane (**kah**-nay) - man
kapu (**kah**-poo) - taboo; forbidden
kaka-roach (**kah**-kah roach) - theft
kaukau (cow-cow) - food
keiki (**kay**-key) - child
kiawe (key-**ah**-vay) - mesquite tree

kokua (ko-**coo**-ah) - help
kona winds (**ko**-nah winds) - winds that blow against the trades
lanai (lah-**nye**) - porch; also island name
lauhala (lau-**hah**-lah) or *hala* (**hah**-lah) - a tree whose leaves are used in weaving
lei (lay) - flower garland
lolo (low-low) - stupid
lomilomi (**low**-me-**low**-me) - massage; also raw salmon
luau (**loo**-ow) - feast
mahalo (mah-**hah**-low) - thank you
mahalo nui loa (mah-**hah**-low **new**-ee **low**-ah) - thank you very much
mahu (**mah**-who) - gay; homosexual
makai (mah-**kye**) - toward the sea
malihini (mah-lee-**hee**-nee) - newcomer; stranger
mauka (**mau**-kah) - toward the mountains
nani (**nah**-nee) - beautiful
ohana (oh-**hah**-nah) - family
okole (oh-**ko**-lay) - rear; ass
okolemaluna (oh-ko-lay-mah-**loo**-nah) - a toast: bottoms up!
ono (**oh**-no) - tastes good
pahoehoe (pah-**hoy**-hoy) - ropy lava
pakalolo (pah-kah-**low**-low) - marijuana
pakiki head (pah-**key**-key head) - stubborn
pali (**pah**-lee) - cliff
paniolo (pah-nee-**oh**-low) - cowboy
pau (pow) - finished; done
pilikia (pee-lee-**key**-ah) - trouble
puka (**poo**-kah) - hole
pupus (**poo**-poos) - hors d'oeuvres
shaka (**shah**-kah) - great; perfect
swell head - angry
tapa (**tap**-ah) - a tree bark which is used as a fabric
wahine (wah-**hee**-nay) - woman
wikiwiki (**wee**-key-**wee**-key) - quickly; in a hurry
you get stink ear - you don't listen well

Honolulu, B.C. (Before Cook)

GEOLOGIC TIME

More than twenty-five million years ago, during an era when mammals were evolving on land, a fissure opened along the Pacific floor. Beneath tons of sea water, at depths where sunlight never penetrated, molten lava poured from the rift. This liquid basalt, oozing from a hot spot in the earth's center, created a crater along the ocean bottom. Then, as the tectonic plate which comprises the ocean floor continued to drift over the hot spot, other craters appeared. Slowly, in the seemingly endless procession of geologic time, volcanic mountains were building. As the Pacific plate continued its continental drifting, a chain of volcanic islands, stretching almost two thousand miles from northwest to southeast, were eventually created.

On the continents it was also a period of terrible upheaval. The Himalayas, Alps, and Andes were rising, but these great chains would reach their peaks long before the Pacific mountains even touched sea level. Not until a few million years ago did these underwater volcanoes break the surface and become islands. By then, present-day plants and animals inhabited the earth, and apes were rapidly evolving into a new species.

For a couple of million more years, the mountains grew. The forces of erosion cut into them, creating knife-edged cliffs and deep valleys like the awesome *pali* which today rises outside Honolulu. Then plants began germinating: mosses and ferns, springing from wind-blown spores, were probably first, followed by seed plants carried by migrating birds and on ocean currents. The steep-walled valleys provided natural greenhouses in which unique species evolved, while transoceanic winds swept insects and other life from the continents. Bays and harbors such as the outstanding anchorage at Honolulu were formed.

Some islands never survived this birth process; the ocean simply washed them away. The first islands that did endure, at the northwestern end of the Hawaiian chain, proved to be the smallest. Today these islands, with the exception of Midway, are barren uninhabited atolls. The volcanoes which rose last, far to the southeast, became the mountainous archipelago which includes Oahu and is generally known to visitors as the Hawaiian Islands.

POLYNESIAN ARRIVAL

The island of Hawaii, less than two hundred miles from Honolulu, was the last mass created in this dramatic upheaval but the first to be inhabited by humans. Around the eighth century, possibly earlier, Polynesians sailing from the Marquesas Islands and later from Tahiti landed near Hawaii's southern tip. In Europe, mariners were rarely venturing outside the Mediterranean Sea, and it would be centuries before Columbus happened upon the New World. Yet in the Pacific, entire families were crossing 2,500 miles of untracked ocean in hand-carved canoes with sails woven from coconut fibers. The boats were awesome structures, catamaran-like vessels with a cabin built on the platform between the wooden hulls. Some were a hundred feet long and could do twenty knots, making the trip to Hawaii in a month.

The Polynesians had originally come from the coast of Asia about three thousand years before. They had migrated through Indonesia, then pressed inexorably eastward, leapfrogging across archipelagoes until they finally reached the last chain, the most remote—Hawaii.

These Pacific migrants were undoubtedly the greatest sailors of their day, and stand among the finest in history. When close to land they could smell it, taste it in the seawater, see it in a lagoon's turquoise reflection on the clouds above an island. They knew 150 stars. From the water color, they determined ocean depths and current directions. They had no charts, no compasses, no sextants; sailing directions were simply recorded in legends and chants. Yet Polynesians discovered the Pacific, from Indonesia to Easter Island, from New Zealand to Hawaii. They made the Vikings and Phoenicians look like landlubbers. Today at Honolulu's Bishop Museum, you can recapture a sense of their undaunted exploits in a series of historical displays.

HAWAIIAN CULTURE

Hawaii, according to Polynesian legend, was discovered by Hawaii-loa, an adventurous sailor who often disappeared on long fishing trips. On one voyage, urged along by his navigator, Hawaii-loa sailed toward the planet Jupiter. He crossed the "many-colored oceans," passed over the "deep-colored sea," and eventually came upon "flaming

Hawaii," a mountainous island chain that spewed smoke and lava.

History is less romantic. The Polynesians who found Hawaii were probably driven from their home islands by war or some similar calamity. They traveled in groups, not as lone rangers, and shared their canoes with dogs, pigs, and chickens with which they planned to stock new lands. Agricultural plants such as coconuts, yams, taro, sugar cane, bananas, and breadfruit were also stowed on board.

Most important, they transported their culture, an intricate system of beliefs and practices developed in the South Seas. After undergoing the stresses and demands of pioneer life, this traditional lifestyle was transformed into a new and uniquely Hawaiian culture.

It was based on a caste system that placed the *alii* or chiefs at the top and the slaves, *kauwas*, on the bottom. Between these two groups were the priests, *kahunas*, and the common people or *makaainanas*. The chiefs, much like feudal lords, controlled all the land and collected taxes from the commoners who farmed it. Oahu and the other islands were divided like pies into wedge-shaped plots, *ahupuaas*, which extended from the ocean to the mountain peaks. In that way, every chief's domain contained fishing spots, village sites, arable valleys, and everything else necessary for the survival of his subjects.

Life centered around the *kapu*, a complex group of regulations which dictated what was sacred or profane. For example, women were not permitted to eat pork or bananas; commoners had to prostrate themselves in the presence of a chief. These strictures were vital to Hawaiian religion; *kapu* breakers were directly violating the will of the gods and could be executed for their actions. And there were a lot of gods to watch out for, many quite vindictive. The four central gods were *Kane*, the creator, *Lono*, the god of agriculture, *Ku*, the war god, and *Kanaloa*, lord of the underworld. They had been born from the sky father and earth mother, and had in turn created many lesser gods and demigods who controlled various aspects of nature.

It was, in the uncompromising termiology of the West, a stone-age civilization. Though the Hawaiians lacked metal tools, the wheel, and a writing system, they managed to include within their short inventory of cultural goods everything necessary to sustain a large population on a chain of small islands. They fashioned fish nets from coconut fibers, made hooks out of bone, shell, and ivory, and raised fish in rock-bound ponds. The men used irrigation in their farming. The women made clothing by pounding mulberry bark into a soft cloth called *tapa*, dyeing elaborate patterns into the fabric. They built peak-roofed thatch huts from native *pili* grass and *lauhala* leaves. The men fought wars with spears, slings, clubs, and daggers; the women used mortars and pestles to pound the roots of the taro plant into *poi*, the islanders' staple food.

The West labeled these early Hawaiians "noble savages." Actually, they often lacked nobility. The Hawaiians were cannibals who sometimes practiced human sacrifice and often used human bait to fish for sharks. They constantly warred among themselves and would mercilessly pursue a retreating army, murdering as many of the vanquished soldiers as possible.

But they weren't savages either. The Hawaiians developed a rich oral tradition of genealogical chants and created beautiful lilting songs to accompany their hula dancing. Their musicians mastered several instruments including the *ukeke* (a single-stringed device resembling a bow), an *ohe* or nose flute, conch shells, rattles, and drums made from gourds, coconut shells, or logs. Their craftsmen produced the world's finest featherwork, weaving thousands of tiny feathers into golden cloaks and ceremonial helmets. The Hawaiians helped develop the sport of surfing. They also swam, boxed, bowled, and devised an intriguing game called *konane*, a cross between checkers and the Japanese game of *go*. They built hiking trails from coral and lava, and created an elemental art form in the images—petroglyphs—which they carved into rocks along the trails.

They also achieved something far more outstanding than their varied arts and crafts, something which the West, with its awesome knowledge and advanced technology, has never duplicated. The Hawaiians created a balance with nature. They practiced conservation, establishing closed seasons on certain fish species and carefully guarding their plant and animal resources. They led a simple life, without the complexities the outside world would eventually thrust upon them. It was a good life; food was plentiful, people were healthy, and the population increased. For a thousand years

A FLOWER *LEI* MEANS *ALOHA*

Aloha, that spirit of friendship and love which Hawaiians have given to the world, finds its purest expression in the flower *lei*. As you arrive or depart the islands, a friend may slip a fragrant wreath across your shoulders, plant a kiss on one cheek, and introduce you to Hawaii's most beautiful custom. Or perhaps you'll attend a wedding, birthday, or other celebration for which islanders traditionally exchange *leis*.

Leis are as old as the islands. According to legend, the maiden Hiiaka originated the custom when she draped a garland over her sister Pele, the goddess of volcanoes. During Hawaii's royal era, *leis* were fashioned from feathers, ferns, and even seaweed. Lacking needle and thread, early Polynesians used stiff blades of grass and banana bark strands to string necklaces.

Today *leis* are sometimes made with shells, paper, and nuts, though most commonly flowers are

the Hawaiians lived in delicate harmony with the elements. It wasn't until the West entered the realm, transforming everything, that the fragile balance was destroyed.

Honolulu, A.D. (After Discovery)

CAPTAIN COOK

They were high islands, rising in the northeast as the sun broke across the Pacific. First one, then a second, and finally, as the tall-masted ships drifted west, a third island loomed before them. Landfall! The British crew was ecstatic. It meant fresh used. You'll find ginger, carnation, and plumeria *leis*, and others entwined with *maile* leaves. *Pikake* (or jasmine) *leis*, strung with buds in the afternoon, blossom in the evening, earning them the nickname "twilight *leis*."

Presenting *leis* has become so important an island practice that May 1 is celebrated every year as *Lei* Day. Each island has its own representative *lei*. On Oahu it is the *ilima*, a delicate flower that varies from yellow to rich orange.

While in Honolulu, the best places to buy *leis* are at the airport, along Maunakea Street downtown, or on South King Street near the University of Hawaii campus. When wearing a flower necklace, place it across the shoulders so it drapes equally in front and back. Afterwards, to maintain its freshness, sprinkle with water, place in a plastic bag, and keep refrigerated.

If you'd like to remember a friend back home, it's easy to airship *leis*. This circle of flowers is a perfect way to say *aloha*. You won't be able to accompany the gift with a kiss, but it will bring a breath of the islands to someone you cherish.

water, tropical fruits, solid ground on which to set their boots, and a chance to carouse with the native women. For their captain, James Cook, it was another in an amazing career of discoveries. The man whom many call history's greatest explorer was about to land in one of the last spots on earth to be discovered by the West.

It was January 1778. Cook had landed on the island of Kauai, little more than a hundred miles northwest of Honolulu. While it would not be until 1792 that another Englishman, Captain William Brown, discovered Honolulu's "fair haven," it was obvious from the beginning that the Hawaiian islands were jewels in the ocean. They were rich in fragrant sandalwood, ripe for agricultural exploitation, and crowded with sea life. Later, when Honolulu was developed as a seaport, it turned out that the greatest resource of all was the archipelago's isolation. For Hawaii was strategically situated between Asia and North America, and Honolulu was one of the few places for thousands of miles to which whalers, merchants, and bluejackets could repair for provisions and rest.

The place which afforded Cook his great discovery also took his life. Within a year of landing in Hawaii, he was slain by natives who had earlier befriended him. Befitting the Britisher's historic stature, his end marked the beginning of an era. He had put the Pacific on the map, his map, probing its expanses and defining its fringes. In Hawaii he ended a thousand years of solitude. The archipelago's geographic isolation, which has always played a crucial role in Hawaii's development, had finally failed to protect it, and a second theme had come into play—the islands' vulnerability. Together with the region's "backwardness," these conditions would now mold Hawaii's history. All in turn would be shaped by another factor, one which James Cook had added to Hawaii's historic equation. The West.

KAMEHAMEHA

The next man whose star would rise above Hawaii was present at Cook's death. Some say he struck the Englishman, others that he took a lock of the great leader's hair and used its residual power, its *mana*, to become king of all Hawaii.

Kamehameha. A tall, muscular, unattractive man with a furrowed face, a lesser chief on the powerful island of Hawaii. In Kamehameha's early years Oahu and the other islands were composed of many fiefdoms. Several kings or great chiefs, continually warring among themselves, ruled individual islands. At times a few kings would carve up one island or a lone king might seize several. Never had one monarch controlled all the islands.

But fresh players had entered the field: Westerners with ample firepower and awesome ships. During the decade following Cook, only a handful had arrived, mostly Englishmen and Americans, and they had not yet won the influence which they soon would wield. However, even a few foreigners were enough to upset the balance of power. They sold weapons and hardware to the great chiefs, making several of them more powerful than any of the others had ever been. War was imminent.

In 1795, Oahu's bold King Kalanikupule killed Captain William Brown in an attempt to commandeer the Englishman's gunboats and turn them against Kamehameha. But Kamehameha had also been arming himself for battle. When two white men had come into his camp in 1790, he gained the military advisers to complement an already expanding arsenal. Within months he had cannonaded Maui. In 1792 Kamehameha had seized the Big Island by inviting his main rival to a peaceful parley, then slaying the hapless chief. By 1795 he had consolidated his control of Maui, grasped Molokai and Lanai, and begun reaching greedily toward Oahu. He struck rapidly, landing near Honolulu's Waikiki district and sweeping inland, forcing his enemies to their deaths over the precipitous cliffs of the Nuuanu Pali, and ending Kalanikupule's rule.

The warrior had become a conqueror. During his reign, Honolulu developed into one of the mid-Pacific's premier harbors, and for several years King Kamehameha ruled the islands from this budding city. During that period he cast a long shadow across Honolulu and all Hawaii, but the event which most dramatically transformed Hawaiian society occurred after his death in 1819.

The kingdom then passed to Kamehameha's son Liholiho, but Kamehameha's favorite wife, Kaahumanu, usurped the power. Liholiho was a prodigal son, dissolute, lacking self-certainty, a drunk. Kaahumanu was a woman for all seasons, a canny politician who combined brilliance with boldness, the feminist of her day.

Following Kamehameha's death, Kaahumanu immediately marched against Hawaii's belief system, trying to topple the old idols. For years she had bristled under a polytheistic religion regulated by taboos, or *kapus*, which severely restricted females. Now Kaahumanu urged the new king, Liholiho, to break a very strict *kapu* by sharing a meal with women. It was a Last Supper, shattering an ancient creed and opening the way for a radically new divinity. As Kaahumanu had willed, the old order collapsed, taking away a vital part of island life and leaving the Hawaiians more exposed than ever to foreign influence.

Already Western practices were gaining hold. Commerce from Honolulu and other ports was booming. There was a fortune to be made dealing sandalwood to China-bound merchants, and the chiefs were forcing the common people to strip Hawaii's forests. The grueling labor might make the chiefs rich, but it gained the commoners little more than a barren landscape. Western diseases struck virulently. The Polynesians in Hawaii, who numbered 300,000 in Cook's time, were extremely susceptible. By 1866 their population would dwindle to less than 60,000. It was a difficult time for the Hawaiian people.

THE MISSIONARIES

Hawaii was not long without religion. The same year that Kaahumanu shattered tradition, a group of New England missionaries boarded the brig *Thaddeus* for a voyage around Cape Horn. It was a young company—many were in their twenties or thirties—which included a doctor, a printer, and several teachers. They were all strict Calvinists, fearful that the Second Coming was at hand and possessed of a mission. They were bound for a strange land called Hawaii, 18,000 miles away.

The delegation arrived in Kailua on the Big Island in 1820 and then spread out, establishing important missions in Honolulu and Lahaina. Soon they were building schools and churches, conducting services in Hawaiian, and converting the natives to Christianity.

In Honolulu they built the Kawaiahao Church, an impressive structure composed of 14,000 coral blocks that stands yet today. Touring contemporary Honolulu, you can also see their Mission Houses, built in the 1820s, which include a prim woodframe edifice that perfectly reflects the architecture of the missionaries' native New England.

Despite their industriousness, the missionaries were soon pitted against other foreigners who were quite willing to let the clerics sing hymns but were damned opposed to permitting them a voice in anything else. Hawaii in the 1820s had become a favorite way station for the whaling fleet. As the sandalwood forests were decimated, the island merchants began looking for other industries. By the 1840s, when over 500 ships a year anchored in Hawaiian ports, whaling had become the islands' economic lifeblood. More American ships visited Hawaii than any other port in the world.

Religion simply could not compete with commerce, and other Westerners were continuously stimulating more business in the islands. In the 1840s and 1850s, when Hawaii adopted a parliamentary form of government and declared Honolulu the capital of the kingdom, American and British fortune hunters were replacing missionaries as government advisers. It was a time when anyone, regardless of ability or morality, could travel to the islands and become a political powerhouse literally overnight.

The situation was no different internationally. Hawaii was subject to the whims and terrors of gunboat diplomacy. The archipelago was solitary and exposed, and Western powers were beginning to eye it covetously. In 1843, a maverick British naval officer, based in Honolulu, annexed Hawaii to the Crown, but the London government later countermanded his actions. Then, in the early 1850s, the threat of American annexation arose. Restless Californians, fresh from the gold fields and hungry for revolution, plotted unsuccessfully in Honolulu. Even the French periodically sent gunboats in to protect their small Catholic minority.

Finally the three powers officially stated that they wanted to maintain Hawaii's national integrity. But independence seemed increasingly unlikely. European countries had already begun claiming other Pacific islands, and with the influx of Yankee missionaries and whalers, Hawaii was being steadily drawn into the American orbit.

MISSIONARY SONS AND ASIAN IMMIGRANTS

There is an old Hawaiian saying that describes the nineteenth century: the missionaries came to do good, and they did very well. Actually the early evangelists, few of whom profited from their work, lived out only half the maxim. Their sons would give the saying its full meaning.

This second generation, quite willing to sacrifice glory for gain, fit neatly into the commercial society which had rendered their fathers irrelevant. They were shrewd, farsighted, young Christians who had grown up in Hawaii and knew both the islands' pitfalls and potentials. Realizing that a one-industry economy based on whaling would never do, they began to develop an alternative industry—sugar. The first plantation was started in 1835, but not until the 1870s did the new industry bloom.

Then, needing laborers to work the fields, they determined to bring immigrant workers from Asia. It was a crucial decision, one that would ramify forever through Hawaiian history and change the very substance of island society. Between 1850 and 1930, 180,000 Japanese, 125,000 Filipinos, 50,000 Chinese, and 20,000 Portuguese immigrated. Disembarking in Honolulu and settling throughout the islands, they transformed Hawaii from a chain of Polynesian islands into one of the world's most varied and dynamic locales, a meeting place of East and West.

The Chinese were the first to come, arriving in 1852 and soon outnumbering the white population. Initially, with their long pigtails and uncommon habits, the Chinese were a joke around the islands. They were poor people from southern China whose lives were directed by clan loyalty. They built schools and worked hard so that one day they could return to their native villages in glory. They were ambitious, industrious, and—ultimately—successful.

In the 1880s, Portuguese began arriving, then in 1886 the sugar planters turned to Japan, with its restricted land mass and burgeoning population. The new immigrants were peasants from Japan's southern islands, raised in an authoritarian, hierarchical culture in which the father was a family dictator and the family was strictly defined by its social status. Like the Chinese, they built schools to protect their heritage and dreamed of returning home someday; but unlike their Asian neighbors, they only married other Japanese. They sent home for "picture brides" and worshipped their ancestors and Emperor. By 1910 the sugar planters had turned to the Philippines for labor. For two decades the Filipinos arrived, seeking their fortunes and leaving their wives behind.

As a result of this extensive immigration, by the late nineteenth century, sugar was king. It had become the center of island economy, the principal fact of life for most islanders. Like the earlier whaling industry, it was drawing Hawaii ever closer to the American sphere. The sugar planters were selling the bulk of their crops in California; having already signed several tariff treaties to protect their American market, they were eager to further strengthen mainland ties. Besides, many sugar planters were second-, third-, and fourth-generation descendants of the New England missionaries; they had a natural affinity for the United States.

Among the Hawaiian people, however, America posed a threat to national sovereignty. Led by their king, David Kalakaua, they became increasingly anticolonialist during the 1870s and 1880s. To symbolize his monarchial stature, Kalakaua built the grand Iolani Palace, an ornate edifice in Honolulu that today represents America's only royal palace.

But not even a castle could protect Kalakaua's kingdom. In 1887, Hawaii's planters and businessmen, backed by a force of well-armed followers, pushed through the "Bayonet Constitution," a document which weakened the king and strengthened the white landowners.

That was only the beginning; once revolution is in the air, it's often difficult to clear the smoke. By 1893 Kalakaua was dead and his sister, Liliuokalani, had succeeded to the throne. She was an audacious leader, proud of her heritage, quick to defend it, and prone to let immediate passions carry her onto dangerous ground. At a time when she should have hung fire, she charged, proclaiming publicly that she would abrogate the new constitution and reestablish a strong monarchy. The businessmen-cum-revolutionaries had the excuse they needed. They struck swiftly, seized government buildings in Honolulu and, with four boatloads of American marines and the support of the American minister, secured the city. Liliuokalani surrendered, and the businessmen soon formed a republic, naming Sanford Dole, a missionary descendant, as president.

THE MODERN WORLD

With the young island republic in their grasp, Dole and his associates fulfilled their ultimate design — Hawaii was annexed by the United States in 1898 and granted territorial status. During the first half of the twentieth century, Honolulu continued to flourish and Waikiki became a favored travel resort. The white-columned Moana Hotel went up in 1901, followed by Hawaii's "Pink Palace," the Royal Hawaiian Hotel, in 1927. Honolulu was rapidly maturing into the capital of the Pacific, a perfect place to mix business with pleasure.

All that ended on December 7, 1941. The Japanese bombers which attacked Pearl Harbor sent shock waves through Hawaii that are still rumbling today. World War II changed all the rules of the game, upsetting the conditions that had determined island history for centuries.

During and after the war, the islands began to catch up with the mainland United States, rapidly acquiring the double-edged qualities of modernity. Hawaii became America's fiftieth state in 1959, Honolulu grew into a vibrant high-rise city, and condominiums mushroomed along Oahu's beaches. Military expenditures boosted the local economy, and with the development of passenger jet service, tourist dollars began to flood the islands. In 1939, only about 500 people flew to Honolulu; now practically four million land every year. Similarly, the island chain's overall population exploded from a half-million just after World War II to almost a million today.

In short, Hawaii and its capital city of Honolulu have arrived. An island chain which slept for centuries has been awakened by the forces of change and risen to become a vital part of the modern world.

KAMEHAMEHA I

CHAPTER II

Discovering Paradise

How to Go

GETTING TO THE ISLANDS

During the nineteenth century, sleek clipper ships sailed from the West Coast to Hawaii in about eleven days. Today you'll be traveling by a less romantic but far swifter conveyance—the jet plane. Rather than days at sea, it will be about five hours in the air from California, nine hours from Chicago, or around eleven hours if you're coming from New York.

There's really nothing easier, or more exciting, than catching a plane to Honolulu. No fewer than eight major airlines—**United, World, Continental, American, Braniff, Northwest Orient, Pan American**, and **Western**—fly regular schedules there from various points in the United States. From Canada, **CP Air** and Western fly to Honolulu.

Among these carriers, my first choice is **United Airlines**. From almost any part of the mainland United States, they provide the most frequent service. United flies non-stop from many cities, and carries approximately half of all the mainlanders visiting Hawaii. Combined with the company's punctuality and professionalism, their frequency of service makes them number one on the trans-Pacific route.

Economically speaking, **World Airways** is the best way to fly to Honolulu. Among the mainland's major carriers, World generally provides the cheapest flights from either the East or West Coasts to the islands. Their flights do tend to run late at times, and the service can be slow, but World does deliver you to the islands, and saves you money in the process.

Whichever carrier you choose, ask for the economy or excursion fare, and try to fly during the week; weekend flights are usually about ten percent higher. To qualify for lower price fares, it is sometimes necessary to book your flight seven days in advance and to stay in the islands a maximum of thirty days. Generally, however, the restrictions are minimal. Children (two to eleven years) can usually fly for two-thirds the regular fare. Each passenger is permitted two large pieces of luggage plus a carry-on bag. Shipping a bike or surfboard will cost extra.

In planning a Hawaiian sojourn one potential money-saver is the **package tour**, which combines air transportation with a hotel room and other amenities. Generally, it is a style of travel that I avoid. However, if you can find a package that provides air transportation, a hotel or condominium accommodation, and a rental car, all at one low price—it might be worth considering. Just try to stay away from the packages that preplan your entire visit, dragging you around on air-conditioned tour buses. Look for the package that provides only the bare necessities, namely transportation and lodging, while allowing you the greatest freedom. As in the case of other travel arrangements, package tours should be booked as far in advance as possible. Since there are numerous companies offering tours, shop around for the best deal.

However you decide to go, be sure to consult a **travel agent**. They are professionals in the field, possessing the latest information on rates and facilities, and their service to you is usually free. Personally, I book almost all my trips through a travel agent, for the simple reason that it saves me time, money, and hassle. Agents generally know the prices for airline and ground facilities, and can book you at the lowest rates; they also will make all the reservations necessary, thus saving you from a series of costly, time-consuming phone calls. Without doubt, a travel agent is the vacationer's best friend.

When to Go

SEASONS

There are two types of seasons in Honolulu, one keyed to tourists and the other to the climate. The peak tourist seasons run from mid-December until Easter, then again from mid-June through Labor Day. Particularly around the Christmas holidays and in August, the visitor centers are crowded. Prices increase, hotel rooms and rental cars become harder to reserve, and everything moves a bit more rapidly.

If you plan to visit the city during these seasons, make reservations several months in advance; actually, it's a good idea to make advance reservations whenever you visit. Without doubt, the off-season is the best time to hit the islands. Not only are hotels more readily available, but beaches and points of interest are also less crowded.

Climatologically, the ancient Hawaiians distinguished between two seasons—*kau*, or summer, and *boo-ilo*, or winter. Summer extends from May to October, when the sun is overhead and the temperatures are slightly higher. Winter brings more variable winds and cooler weather.

The important rule to remember about the beautiful weather in the Hawaiian islands is that it changes very little from season to season but varies dramatically from place to place. The average yearly temperature is about 75^0, and during the coldest weather in January and the warmest in August, the thermometer rarely moves more than 5^0 or 6^0 in either direction. Similarly, sea water temperatures range comfortably between 74^0 and 80^0 year-round.

Of course, if you travel from Honolulu to the mountains, you'll find that the temperature drops about 3^0 for every thousand feet you ascend. And over on the windward side of Oahu, where the prevailing breezes often bring clouds, you'll encounter more precipitation. But in Honolulu, sheltered by the mountains, you can usually count on warm, sunny weather.

A key aspect to this luxurious semitropical environment is the trade wind, which blows with welcome regularity from the northeast, providing a natural form of air-conditioning. When the trades stop blowing, they are sometimes replaced by *kona* winds carrying rain and humid weather from the southwest. These are most frequent in winter, when the islands receive their heaviest rainfall.

CALENDAR OF EVENTS

Something else to consider in planning when to visit Hawaii is the amazing lineup of annual cultural events. For a thumbnail idea of what's happening when, check the calendar below. You might just find that special occasion to climax an already dynamic vacation.

JANUARY

Mid-January or February: The month-long **Narcissus Festival** begins with the Chinese New Year. During the weeks of festivities there are open houses, street parties, and parades in Honolulu's Chinatown.

FEBRUARY

Mid-February: The four-day **Haleiwa Sea Spree** on Oahu's North Shore, features surfing championships, outrigger canoe races, ancient Hawaiian Olympic sports, and an around-the-island bicycle race.

Late February through March: The Japanese community celebrates its **Cherry Blossom Festival** in Honolulu with tea ceremonies, *Kabuki* theatre presentations, martial arts demonstrations, and crafts exhibits.

MARCH

During March: Island musicians perform at Waikiki's Kapiolani Park in the **Hawaiian Song Festival and Song Composing Contest**. Hawaiian school children also compete in Honolulu in the **Kamehameha Schools Annual Song Contest**. For tickets to the latter, write in advance to Kamehameha Schools, Kapalama Heights, Honolulu, Oahu, HI 96817.

March 26: Major festivities on Oahu mark the **Prince Kuhio Festival**, commemorating the birthdate of Prince Jonah Kuhio Kalanianaole, Hawaii's first delegate to the U.S. Congress.

APRIL

Early April: Buddhist temples all over Oahu mark **Buddha Day**, the luminary's birthday, with special services. Included among the events are pageants, dances, and flower festivals.

Easter Sunday: **Sunrise services** are performed at the National Memorial Cemetery in Punchbowl Crater.

MAY

May 1: **Lei Day** is celebrated on all the islands by people wearing flower *leis* and colorful Hawaiian garb. In Oahu's Kapiolani Park there are pageants and concerts.

Mid-May: **Fiesta Filipina**, a month-long celebration of

Filipino culture—songs, folk dances, and craft exhibits—begins on Oahu.

Last Monday: School children commemorate **Memorial Day** by decorating the graves at the National Memorial Cemetery in Punchbowl Crater.

JUNE

During June: Canoeists vie on Oahu in the 100-mile **Around-the-Island Canoe Race**.

June 11: **Kamehameha Day**, honoring Hawaii's first king, is celebrated with parades, chants, hula dances, foot races, and exhibits.

JULY

During July and August: On Oahu and the other islands, Buddhists perform colorful **Bon Dances** every weekend to honor the dead.

Fourth of July: **Independence Day** is celebrated with an array of fireworks.

Mid-July: In odd-numbered years, the vaunted **TransPacific Yacht Race** finishes just offshore from Honolulu.

AUGUST

During August, on consecutive Sundays: Local artists perform at the **Hula Festival** and the **Ukelele Festival** in Waikiki's Kapiolani Park.

During August: The dramatic **Hawaii State Surfing Championships** and **Bodysurfing Championships** are held on Oahu.

SEPTEMBER

Late September and during October: The highlight of Hawaii's cultural season is the **Aloha Week** festival, a series of week-long celebrations featuring parades, street parties, and pageants. Each week a different island stages the festival, and the entire sequence ends with a **Molokai-to-Oahu Canoe Race**.

OCTOBER

During October: The **Orchid and Flower Show** in

Honolulu presents thousands of orchids and other tropical plants.

NOVEMBER

Late November and early December: The world's greatest surfers compete on Oahu's North Shore in a series of contests including the **Smirnoff Pro-Am Surfing Championships, Men's World Cup, Women's World Cup**, and the **Duke Kahanamoku Surfing Classic**. With thirty-foot waves and prize money topping $50,000, these are spectacular events.

DECEMBER

Early December: The Christmas season begins in Honolulu with the **Festival of Trees**, featuring colorful decorations and beautiful native trees.

Early December: Buddha's enlightenment is commemorated on all the islands with **Bodhi Day** ceremonies and religious services.

Early December: Runners by the thousands turn out for the **Honolulu Marathon**.

December 7: **Memorial services** are performed aboard the U.S.S. Arizona Memorial in Pearl Harbor.

Mid-December: The **Kailua Madrigal Singers Annual Christmas Concert** is staged on Oahu.

Late December: The **Makaha Surfing Championships**, with events for top men and women surfers, are held on Oahu.

December 31: **New Year's Eve** is celebrated with ear-boggling demonstrations of fireworks.

What to Take

When I get ready to pack for a trip, I sit down and make a list of everything I'll need. It's a very slow, exact procedure: I look in closets, drawers, and shelves, and run through in my mind the activities in which I'll participate, determining which items are required for each. After all the planning is complete and when I have the entire inventory collected in one long list, I sit for a minute or two, basking in my wisdom and forethought.

Then I tear the heck out of the list, cut out the ridiculous items I'll never use, halve the number of spares among the necessary items, and reduce the entire contents of my suitcase to the bare essentials.

Before I developed this packing technique, I once traveled overland from London to New Delhi carrying two suitcases and a knapsack. I lugged those blasted bundles onto trains, buses, jitneys, taxis, and rickshaws. When I reached Turkey I started shipping things home, but by then I was buying so many market goods that it was all I could do to keep even.

I ended up carrying so much junk that one day when I was sardined in a crowd pushing its way onto an Indian train, someone managed to pick my pocket. When I felt the wallet slipping out, not only was I unable to chase the culprit — I was so weighed down with baggage that I couldn't even turn around to see who was robbing me!

I'll never travel that way again, and neither should you. Particularly when visiting Hawaii, where the weather is mild, you should pack very light. The airlines permit two suitcases and a carry-on bag; try to take one suitcase and maybe one accessory bag that can double as a beach bag. Dress styles are very informal in the islands, and laundromats are frequent, so you don't need a broad range of clothing items, and you'll require very few extras among the essential items.

Remember, you're packing for a semitropical climate. Take along a sweater or light jacket for the mountains, and a poncho to protect against rain. But otherwise, all that travelers in Hawaii require are shorts, bathing suits, lightweight slacks, short-sleeved shirts and blouses, and summer dresses or *muumuus*. Rarely do visitors require sport jackets or formal dresses. Wash-and-wear fabrics are the most convenient.

For footwear, I suggest soft, comfortable shoes. Low-cut hiking boots or tennis shoes are preferable for hiking; for beachgoing, there's nothing as good as sandals.

There are several other items to squeeze in the corners of your suitcase — suntan lotion, sunglasses, a towel, and of course, your copy of *Hidden Honolulu*. You might also consider packing a mask, fins, and snorkel, and possibly a camera.

If you plan on camping, you'll need most of the equipment required for mainland overnighting. In Hawaii you can get along quite comfortably with a lightweight tent and sleeping bag. You'll also need a knapsack, canteen, camp stove and fuel, mess kit, first-aid kit (with insect repellent, water purification tablets, and Chapstick), toilet kit, a pocket knife, hat, waterproof matches, flashlight, and ground cloth.

How to Deal With...

CAR RENTALS

Renting a car is as easy in Honolulu as anywhere. The city supports countless rental agencies, which compete fiercely with one another in price and quality of service. So before renting, shop around: check the listings in this book, and also look for the special temporary offers that many rental companies sometimes feature.

There are several facts to remember when renting a car. First of all, a major credit card is very helpful; if you lack one, you'll often have to leave a cash deposit on the car. Also, some agencies don't rent at all to people under twenty-five. Regardless of your age, many companies charge about $3 a day extra for insurance. The insurance is optional, but if you don't take it you're liable for the first several hundred dollars in accident damage. So before leaving home, check to see how much coverage your personal insurance policy provides for rental cars.

Rates fluctuate with the season; slack tourist seasons are great times for good deals. Also, three-day, weekly, and monthly rates are almost always cheaper than daily rentals; cars with standard shifts are generally less than automatics; and sedans are more economical than the larger four-door models. You may also be given the option of a flat daily rate or a rate keyed to the number of miles driven. Take the flat rate — it will almost always prove less expensive. Whichever you choose, you'll have to buy your own gas.

CONDOMINIUM LIVING

Many people visiting Honolulu, especially those traveling with families, find that condominiums are often cheaper than hotels. While some hotel rooms come equipped with kitchenettes, few provide all the amenities of condominiums. A condo, in essence, is an apartment away from home. Designed as studio, one-, two-, or three-bedroom apartments, they come equipped with full kitchen facilities and complete kitchenware collections. Many also feature washer-dryers, dishwashers, air-conditioning, color televisions, lanais, and community swimming pools. Utilizing the kitchen will save considerably on your food bill; by sharing the accommodations among several people, you'll also cut your lodging bill.

MAIL

If you're staying in a particular establishment during your visit, you can usually have personal mail sent there. Otherwise, **American Express** will hold mail for no charge at its Honolulu office. For a $3 charge they will foward it to you. If you do decide to use their facilities, have mail addressed in care of American Express, 2222 Kalakaua Avenue, Honolulu, Oahu, HI 96815. If you don't use this service, your only other recourse is to have mail sent to a particular **post office** in care of general delivery.

VISITOR INFORMATION

The **Hawaii Visitors Bureau**, a privately-funded agency, is a valuable resource from which to obtain free information on Hawaii. With offices nationwide and branches on each of the four largest islands, the Bureau can help plan your trip and then offer advice once you reach Hawaii.

The Honolulu office is located at 2270 Kalakaua Avenue (923-1811). On the mainland, you can contact the Hawaii Visitors Bureau at the following offices: on the West Coast — at 3440 Wilshire Boulevard, Los Angeles, CA 90010 (213-385-5301), or at 209 Post Street, San Francisco, CA 94108 (415-392-8173); in the Midwest — at 410 North Michigan Avenue, Chicago, IL 60611 (312-944-6694); and on the East Coast — 609 Fifth Avenue, New York, NY 10017 (212-759-3655).

Another excellent resource is the **Hawaii State Library Service.** With a network of libraries on all the islands, this government agency provides facilities that can be used by residents and non-residents alike. The libraries are good places to find light beach-reading material as well as books on Hawaii. Visitors can check out books by simply signing for them.

BEING DISABLED

The **Commission on the Handicapped** is publishing a survey of the city, county, and federal parks in Hawaii that are accessible to disabled people. For information, contact the Commission at 335 Merchant St. #215, Honolulu, Oahu, HI 96813. They have a handy guide available, "The Aloha Guide to Accessibility," with information on each island, including parks.

Another valuable information resource is **Rollin' On: A Wheelchair Guide to U.S. Cities** by Maxine H. Atwater. Honolulu is one of the cities described in this book, which can be obtained from Dodd, Mead & Company, 79 Madison Avenue, New York, NY 10016.

For cars equipped for disabled drivers, check with **Wiki Wiki Wheels** (listed in the section on car rentals).

CHAPTER III

Honolulu: The Good Life

Transportation

ARRIVAL

There's one airport on Oahu and it's a behemoth. **Honolulu International Airport** is a Pacific crossroads, an essential link between North America and Asia. It includes all the comforts of a major airport. Here you can check your bags or rent a locker; fuel up at a restaurant, coffee shop, or cocktail lounge; shop at any of several stores; or shower.

To cover the eight or so miles into town, it's possible to hire a cab for $8, plus a small charge for each bag. **Grayline** (922-4011) runs a shuttle service to Waikiki hotels for $4. And city bus #8 travels through downtown Honolulu and Waikiki. This is the cheapest transportation, but you're only allowed to carry on baggage that fits on your lap. So, unless you're traveling very light, you'll have to use another conveyance.

CAR RENTALS

There are a few things Honolulu does not lack for, such as sand, water—and rental car agencies. Wherever you look it seems someone is trying to rent you a set of wheels. But driver beware! Because of the competition, some of Honolulu's rental agents are worse than used-car dealers. If you're not careful, you could wind up with an unwashed auto that runs poorly and is spotted with litter.

I once rented a car which sputtered to a halt after several days. When I tucked my head under the hood looking for trouble, I discovered the engine lacked an air filter. The carburetor had been breathing dirt, sand, and moisture all across the island! So check your vehicle carefully before leaving the lot, and insist on a spotless car that's been recently tuned and is ready to roll.

When you do finally get out on the road, keep in mind that Hawaiian drivers are extremely polite. They will often yield the right of way or wave you into their lane. A return thank you wave is the general custom. Regardless of the traffic situation, *honking* is considered extremely rude. You won't hear many traffic horns in paradise.

At the airport, **National Car Rental** (836-2655), **Hertz** (836-2511), **Avis** (836-5511), and **Budget Rent-A-Car** (922-3600) all have booths. Although conveniently located, these agencies usually charge a little more for their cars.

Several agencies outside the airport offer low rates and provide pick-up service when your plane arrives. Foremost among these is **Wiki Wiki Wheels** (836-1974; or from the mainland, 800-367-2631). Run by an enterprising fellow named Gary Tiller, Wiki Wiki was once located only on Kauai, but has expanded dramatically and now also services Oahu, Hawaii, and Maui. At its Honolulu facility, Wiki Wiki offers everything from compacts to Mustangs, station wagons to convertibles. There are also jeeps available. Personally, I usually opt for stick-shift compacts as they're the most economical.

In addition to Wiki Wiki Wheels, several other outfits provide airport pick-up service. These include **Tropical Rent-A-Car** (836-1041), **Thrifty Rent-A-Car** (836-2388), **Holiday Rent-A-Car** (833-0086), **Val's U-Drive** (955-0720), **Five-O Rent-A-Car** (836-1028), and **Hawaii Rent-A-Car** (836-2561).

There are many other Honolulu-based companies offering very low rates but providing no pick-up service at the airport. I've never found the inconvenience worth the savings. There you are—newly arrived from the mainland, uncertain about your environment, anxious to check in at the hotel—and you're immediately confronted with the Catch-22 of getting to your car. Do you rent a vehicle in which to pick up your rental car? Take a bus? What do you do with your bags meanwhile?

Nevertheless, if your budget is of primary importance, consider one of the following cheaper but less convenient outfits: **A-Plus Rent-A-Car** (923-9865), **United Car**

Rental (922-4605), **AMC Rent-A-Car System** (946-8311), **ABC Rent-A-Car** (488-3335), **Continental Rent-A-Car Systems** (922-4614), **Honolulu Ford** (531-0491), **VIP Car Rental** (946-1671), **Ford Rent-A-Car** (487-3811), or **Maxi Car Rental System** (523-1952).

If you want a convertible, you can drive away a top-down Mustang from **Convertible Rentals** (923-4131).

JEEP RENTALS

United Car Rental (2352 Kalakaua Avenue; 922-4605) provides jeeps for $34.95 a day.

MOTOR SCOOTER AND MOTORCYCLE RENTALS

Aloha Funway Rentals (1982 Kalakaua Avenue; 955-5886) rents scooters, motorcycles, mopeds, and roller skates. **Leisure Bikes** (2025 Kalakaua Avenue; 955-3705) rents mopeds. Call for rates.

PUBLIC TRANSPORTATION

Oahu has an excellent bus system which runs regularly to points all over the island and provides convenient service throughout Honolulu. Many, many of the beaches, hotels, restaurants, and points of interest are just a bus ride away. It's even possible to pop your money in the fare box and ride around the entire island.

TheBus carries almost 200,000 people daily, loading them into any of 300 yellow-and-orange vehicles that rumble along city streets and country roads from 5 a.m. until midnight.

If you stay in Waikiki you'll inevitably be sardined into a #8 bus for the ride through Honolulu's tourist mecca. Many bus drivers are Hawaiian; I saw some hysterical scenes on the #8 when tourists waited anxiously for their stop to be called, only to realize they couldn't understand the driver's pidgin. Hysterical, that is, after those early days when *I* was the visitor with the furrowed brow.

For information on bus routes call **TheBus** at 531-1611. And remember, the only carry-on luggage permitted is baggage small enough to fit on your lap.

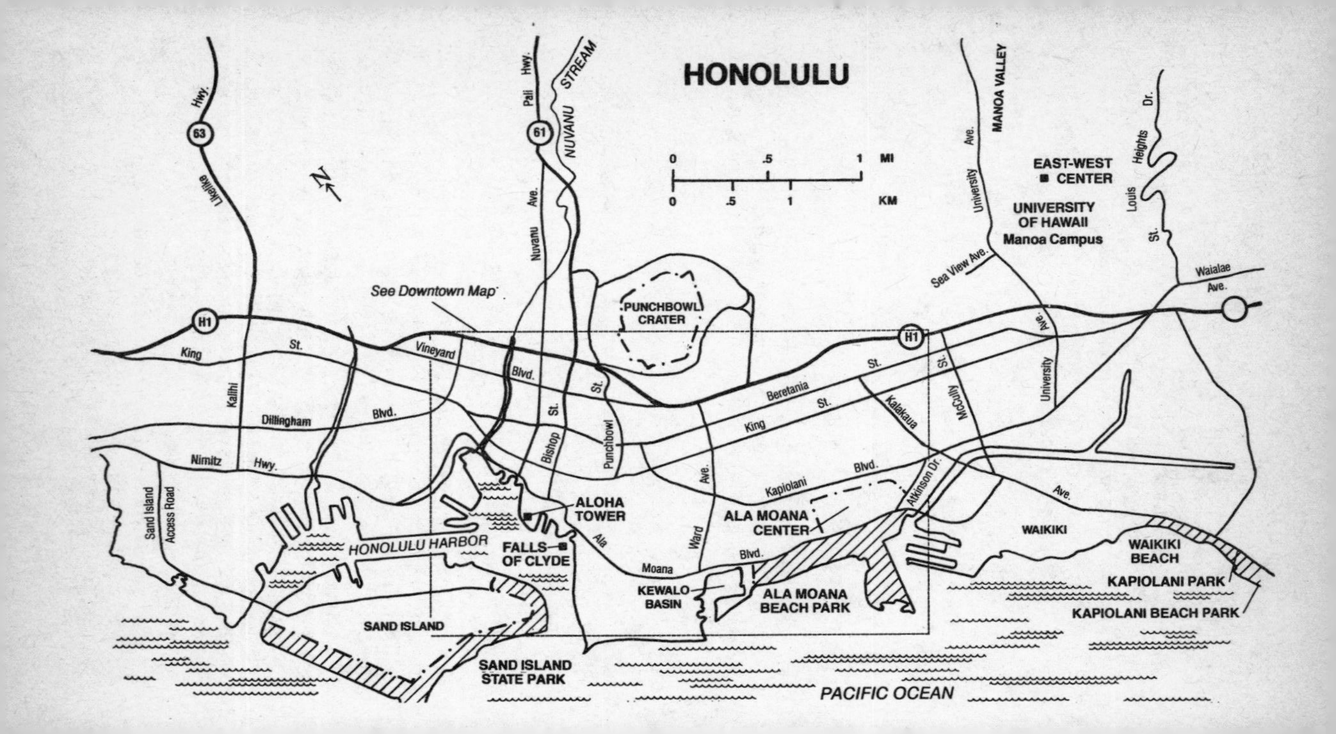
HONOLULU
0 .5 1 MI
0 .5 1 KM
N
Hwy.
63
Likelike
Pali Hwy.
61
Nuuanu Ave.
NUUANU STREAM
H1
King St.
Vineyard Blvd.
Kalihi
Dillingham Blvd.
Nimitz Hwy.
Sand Island Access Road
See Downtown Map
Bishop St.
Punchbowl St.
PUNCHBOWL CRATER
Beretania St.
King St.
Kalakaua
McCully St.
University Ave.
Kapiolani Blvd.
Ward Ave.
Ala Moana Blvd.
Atkinson Dr.
Ave.
MANOA VALLEY
Sea View Ave.
EAST-WEST CENTER
UNIVERSITY OF HAWAII
Manoa Campus
Louis Heights Dr.
St.
Waialae Ave.
ALOHA TOWER
FALLS OF CLYDE
HONOLULU HARBOR
SAND ISLAND
SAND ISLAND STATE PARK
KEWALO BASIN
ALA MOANA CENTER
ALA MOANA BEACH PARK
WAIKIKI
WAIKIKI BEACH
KAPIOLANI PARK
KAPIOLANI BEACH PARK
PACIFIC OCEAN

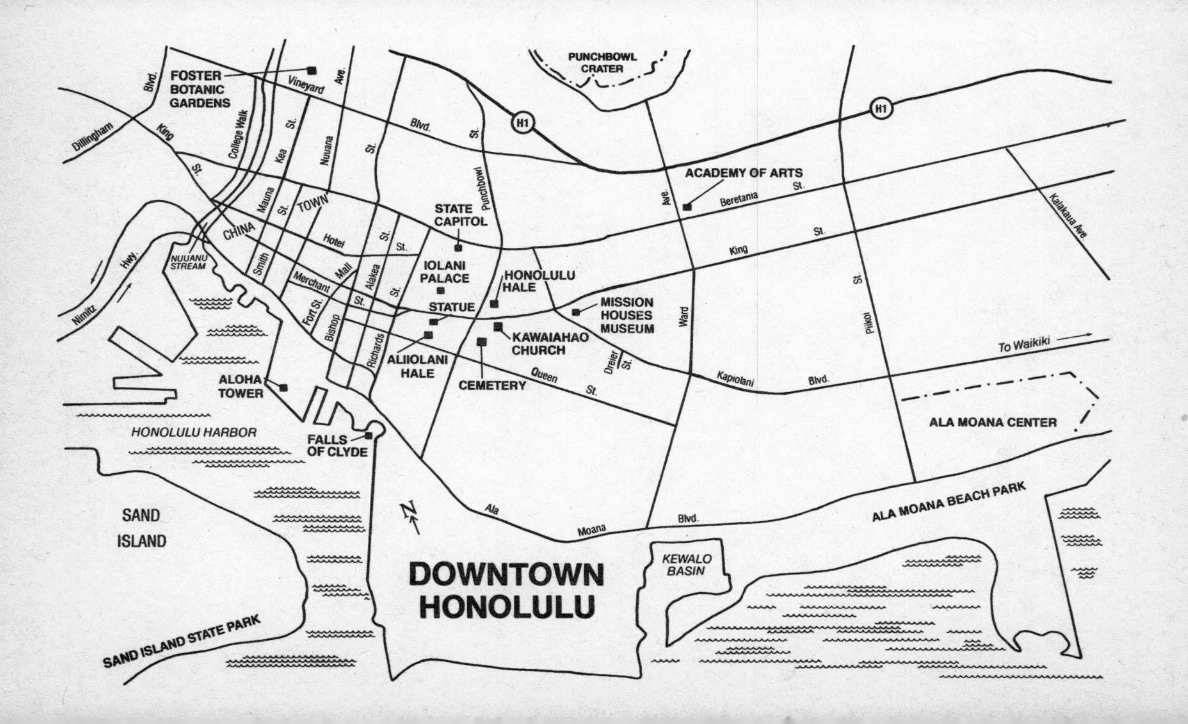
DOWNTOWN HONOLULU
FOSTER BOTANIC GARDENS
PUNCHBOWL CRATER
ACADEMY OF ARTS
STATE CAPITOL
IOLANI PALACE
STATUE
ALIIOLANI HALE
HONOLULU HALE
KAWAIAHAO CHURCH
CEMETERY
MISSION HOUSES MUSEUM
ALOHA TOWER
FALLS OF CLYDE
NUUANU STREAM
HONOLULU HARBOR
SAND ISLAND
SAND ISLAND STATE PARK
KEWALO BASIN
ALA MOANA BEACH PARK
ALA MOANA CENTER
To Waikiki
Kalakaua Ave.
H1
Beretania St.
King St.
Kapiolani Blvd.
Ala Moana Blvd.
Ward Ave.
Piikoi St.
Queen St.
Dreier St.
Punchbowl St.
Richards St.
Alakea St.
Bishop St.
Mall
Fort St.
Merchant St.
Hotel St.
Nuuana Ave.
Vineyard Blvd.
Kea St.
Mauna St.
Smith
College Walk
CHINA TOWN
King St.
Dillingham Blvd.
Nimitz Hwy.
N

In Waikiki you might want to check out the **pedicabs**. These three-wheeled rickshaws, pedaled by young and often street-savvy drivers, are expensive but entertaining conveyances. Several dollars will carry you from one place in Waikiki to another. Even if you decide not to ride around in this grand colonial style, you'll find the drivers are good sources of information. Many know the local scene intimately.

BICYCLING

Oahu is blessed with excellent roads, well-paved, and usually flat, and cursed with heavy traffic. About three-quarters of Hawaii's population lives here, and it sometimes seems that every person owns a car.

Honolulu can be a cycler's nightmare, but outside the city the traffic is somewhat lighter. And Oahu drivers, accustomed to tourists driving mopeds, are relatively conscious of bicyclists.

Keep in mind that the east coast is the wet side, the north shore's slightly drier, and the south and west coasts are driest of all. And remember, ripoffs are a frequent fact of life on Oahu. Leaving your bike unlocked is asking for a long walk back.

If you'd like a little two-wheeled company, check out the **Hawaii Bicycling League** (Box 4403, Honolulu, Oahu, HI 96813), which regularly sponsors bike hikes.

RENTALS

Aloha Funway Rentals (1984 Kalakaua Avenue; 955-5886) in Waikiki and **Bike Stop Sports Center** (87-066 Farrington Highway, Maili; 696-4186) rent bicycles. The latter also sells and repairs them.

REPAIRS

The following shops do repair work, plus sell bikes and accessories; **Eki Cyclery** (Ala Moana Center, Honolulu; 946-5444), **The Bike Shop** (1149 South King Street, Honolulu; 531-7071), **Kailua Bike Shop** (354 Hahani Street, Kailua; 261-9213), and **Wahiawa Cyclery** (203 South Kamehameha Highway, Wahiawa; 621-6220).

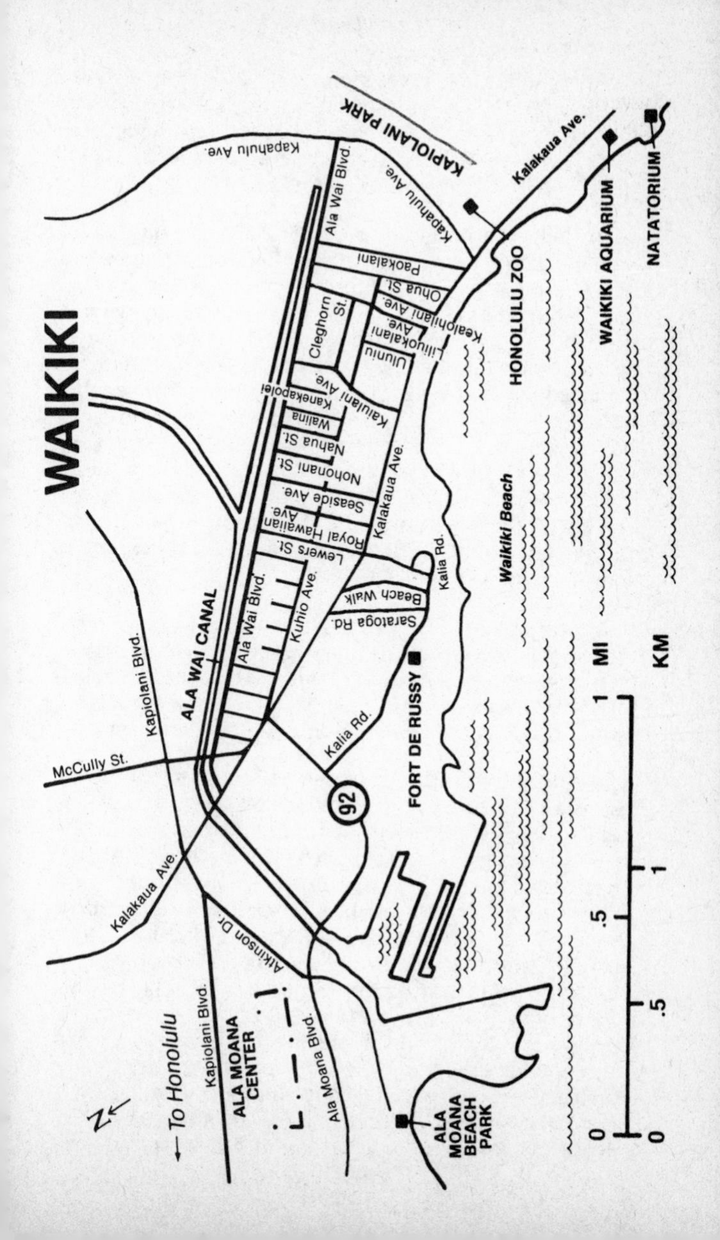
WAIKIKI
To Honolulu
N
Kapiolani Blvd.
ALA MOANA CENTER
Ala Moana Blvd.
ALA MOANA BEACH PARK
Atkinson Dr.
Kalakaua Ave.
McCully St.
Kapiolani Blvd.
92
ALA WAI CANAL
Ala Wai Blvd.
Kuhio Ave.
Kalia Rd.
FORT DE RUSSY
Saratoga Rd.
Beach Walk
Kalia Rd.
Lewers St.
Royal Hawaiian Ave.
Seaside Ave.
Nohonani St.
Nahua St.
Walina
Kanekapolei
Kaiulani Ave.
Kalakaua Ave.
Cleghorn St.
Uluniu
Liliuokalani Ave.
Kealohilani Ave.
Ohua St.
Paoakalani
Ala Wai Blvd.
Kapahulu Ave.
Kapahulu Ave.
KAPIOLANI PARK
Kalakaua Ave.
Waikiki Beach
HONOLULU ZOO
WAIKIKI AQUARIUM
NATATORIUM
MI
0
.5
1
KM
0
.5
1

Hotels

In Honolulu the hotel scene can be described in one word—Waikiki. This vacation mecca is chockablock with facilities, ranging from efficiency apartments to world-class resorts. Everyone from budget traveler to big spender seems inevitably to locate the perfect spot here.

To help you decide on a place to stay, I've divided the accommodations into four categories. Budget hotels generally price around $20 per night for two people; the rooms are clean and comfortable, but lack luxury. The moderately priced hotels run slightly higher, but often provide larger rooms, plusher furniture, and more attractive surroundings. At a deluxe hotel you can expect to spend about $40 double. You'll check in to a spacious, well-appointed room with all modern facilities; downstairs the lobby will be a fashionable affair, and you'll usually see a restaurant, lounge, and a cluster of shops. Waikiki's ultra-deluxe hotels number among the finest anywhere. The ambience is alluring, the rooms elegant, and the service outstanding. Prices, needless to say, are as dazzling as the surroundings.

Venturing out from Waikiki, be you a budgeter or high-roller, you'll discover relatively few hotels. Anyone interested in parking their bags elsewhere will find Greater Honolulu hotels listed later in this chapter; establishments located beyond Honolulu are described in a subsequent chapter.

In selecting a hotel, there are several points to remember. First of all, try to make reservations as far in advance as possible. This is particularly true from Christmas until Easter and during summer months, when Honolulu is especially popular. Keep in mind that you can save money by booking a room with a kitchenette (making it possible to supplement costly restaurant food with home-cooked meals). Other economizing techniques involve settling for a room with a mountain rather than an ocean view, or choosing a hotel that's located away from the water. Waikiki has three major thoroughfares, all of which parallel the beach: Kalakaua Avenue straddles the waterfront and hosts the area's premier hotels; Kuhio Avenue is located one block inland; and Ala Wai Boulevard sits a few blocks away, facing the mountains. Near the latter two streets are situated Waikiki's less costly hotels.

Whatever you decide upon, you'll doubtless discover that hoteliers in this Pacific paradise are endowed with a generous share of that old *aloha* spirit. Happy hotel hunting!

WAIKIKI HOTELS

Waikiki Budget Hotels: While it may no longer be the simple country retreat it was at the century's turn, Waikiki does have one advantage: believe it or not, it's a great place to find low-rent hotels. A lot of the cozy old hostelries have been torn down and replaced with high-rises, but a few have escaped the urban assault. Some of those skyscrapers, too, are cheaper than you might think. So let's take a look at some of the better bargains Waikiki has to offer.

The **Malihini Hotel** (217 Saratoga Road; 923-9644) will give you a feel for Honolulu's earlier low-rise era. An attractive complex which spreads out instead of up, this twenty-eight-unit hotel is just a short stroll from the beach. Though pretty on the outside, its sparse furnishings, scant decoration, and cinder-block walls give a vacant feel to the place. But the studios ($17 double, $20 to $30 deluxe) are spacious and come equipped with kitchenettes. The one-bedroom apartments ($28 double, $40 deluxe) will sleep up to five people.

Also conveniently located a block from Waikiki Beach, **Waikiki Terrace Apartment Hotel** (339 Royal Hawaiian Avenue; 923-3253) has thirty-two units in its slightly run-down complex. All have fully-equipped kitchenettes and rent for $18 to $24 double, depending on room size. Rooms are clean, comfortable, and modestly furnished, with laundry facilities, weekly maid service, and rental parking spaces available. There's some street noise. I recently stayed here for a week and give the place a guarded recommendation.

Sizewise, the last of the least is the **Edmunds Hotel Apartment** (2411 Ala Wai Boulevard; 923-8381). This twelve-unit establishment, situated a long walk from the beach on a noisy street, has a lovely view of the mountains. The rooms are clean and comfortable, but less than chic. All have kitchenettes and televisions. Studios rent for $14 single, $16 double; one-bedroom apartments are $16 single, $18 double.

Rising higher from the ground, while still keeping costs low, is the **Royal Grove Hotel** (151 Uluniu Avenue; 923-7691), a six-story, eighty-five-unit establishment. If you can get past the garish pink exterior here, you'll find the rooms more tastefully designed. All are comfortably furnished, and some are decorated with attractive Japanese wall-hangings. There are televisions, telephones, and carpeting in many of the higher-priced rooms upstairs, plus an almond-shaped pool and spacious lobby downstairs. Rents vary according to which wing of this sprawling building your bags are parked in. A standard room with kitchenette begins at $22.50 double; a one-bedroom apartment starts at $36. (From mid-December until the end of April rooms are about $2 more.)

The **Pacific Prince Hotel** (415 Nahua Street; 922-4666) was once a college dormitory. Today it's a ten-story hotel with a comfortable lobby and small almond-shaped swimming pool. The standard rooms are small, blandly decorated, and equipped with mini-kitchenettes (two-burner stove and a refrigerator, but no oven or sink). They rent for $19 single and $22 double. (The prices increase slightly from November 20 through April 15.) Located near the beach, this hotel also has one- and two-bedroom apartments available.

The cheapest place for men in Waikiki is the **YMCA Central Branch** (401 Atkinson Drive; 941-3344). It's handily situated across the street from Ala Moana Center and a block from the beach. And you're welcome to use the gym, pool, saunas, television room, and coffee shop. Of course, you must abide by the Y's strictures—no liquor or visitors and quiet hours after 10 p.m. You can also expect the usual Y ambience—long sterile hallways leading to an endless series of identical, cramped, uncarpeted rooms. But at $11 single, $19 double (or $13 single, $23 double with private bath), the prices are unique.

If you're willing to sacrifice intimacy, you may find that the **Coral Seas Hotel** (250 Lewers Street; 923-3881) is the best deal in Waikiki. This seven-story hostelry, located just a hundred yards from the beach, has rooms for $18 single, $20 double. They are appealing accommodations with air-conditioning, telephones, wall-to-wall carpeting, and small lanais. For $20 single, $22 double, add a mini-kitchenette to the list of extras. If you want to experience the Waikiki scene, this is the place. The Coral Seas Hotel is at the heart of the action, and has a pool.

Waikiki Moderately Priced Hotels: There are two places in this category that I particularly recommend. Both are small, intimate, and close to the beach. First is the

Hale Pua Nui (228 Beachwalk; 923-9693), a family-operated home away from home. There are twenty-two studio apartments here, each spacious, well-furnished, and cross-ventilated. The rooms are quaintly decorated, carpeted, and equipped with telephones and kitchenettes. The personalized service you receive from owners Paul and Fay Heady makes the Hale Pua Nui an ideal vacation spot. Prices for two people range from $28.50 to $32.50 depending on location within the building.

The second is **Kai Aloha Apartment Hotel** (235 Saratoga Road; 923-6723) just around the corner. Here intimacy is combined with modern convenience: each room has air-conditioning, an all-electric kitchen, radio, telephone, and carpeting. Studio apartments, renting for $32 double, have lovely rattan furniture and are attractively decorated with old drawings and paintings. The one-bedroom apartments are $39 double and will comfortably sleep four people for $42 a night.

Venture Isle Hotel Apartments (2467 Cleghorn Street; 923-6363) is another small, personalized place. Set on a quiet street and surrounded by potted plants, it's weather-beaten but quaint. Spacious studio apartments, featuring a curtained-off area perfect for a third sleeper, are $25 double ($20 during April, May, September, and October). Slightly larger one-bedroom apartments are $35 double ($30 during the off-season). All are decorated in a funky but imaginative style with paintings and drawings; all have separate kitchenettes.

In the very heart of Waikiki is the **Edgewater Hotel** (2168 Kalia Road; 922-6424). Located a stone's skip from the beach, this 180-unit colossus offers excellent accommodations at low prices. Each room comes with telephone, carpeting, and a shared lanai. The decor is bland but the furniture comfy. Downstairs is an open-air lobby with adjoining restaurant and pool. The cost? $20 single, $22 double, for a standard room. Deluxe rooms with kitchenettes are $32 single, $34 double.

White Sands Garden Hotel (431 Nohonani Street; 923-7336) is more expensive but also more fashionable. This is a modern, attractive complex of three low-slung buildings surrounding a garden and swimming pool. The rooms—from $35 single, $39 double—come with all-electric kitchenette, telephone, color television, and air-conditioning. Quite posh for the price.

Hotel hunting can be an exhausting sport in Waikiki during the peak tourist seasons, so I'll mention some other places you can check if you are shut out at the preferred hotels. All provide adequate accommodations but don't measure up to my favorites.

If you'd like to stay directly across the street from the beach, check into the **Waikiki Circle Hotel** (2464 Kalakaua Avenue; 923-1571). This fourteen-story hotel-in-the-round has rooms starting at $20 single, $22 double (prices rise with the floor level). Most have an ocean view, which is the main advantage here. The rooms convey a college ambience: the twin beds (you have to specially request a double bed) roll under bolsters to eke out a bit more living space, and the bathrooms are barely large enough for a toothbrush. I'd sooner walk an extra block to the beach.

Waikiki Holiday Apartment Hotel (450 Lewers Street; 923-0245), a ten-story high-rise, has accommodations for $18 double ($24 with a kitchenette). They're postage-stamp-sized rooms with the tiniest beds I've ever seen. Each room has a small lanai, telephone, and wall-to-wall carpeting; all are air-conditioned. Pool, cocktail lounge, free parking.

If the **Waikiki Surf Hotel** (2200 Kuhio Avenue; 923-7671) has no space in its central facility, they can probably fit you into one of their two other buildings. All are located in central Waikiki. Rooms are priced moderately at $20 single, $22 double ($24 and $26, respectively, with a kitchenette). They're adequately, if unimaginatively, decorated and come with television, air-conditioning, telephone, and lanai.

The **Coral Reef Hotel** (2299 Kuhio Avenue; 922-1262 or toll-free 800-367-5124) has studio units in its Garden Wing across the street from the main hotel. These have televisions, telephones, air-conditioners, and mini-kitchenettes. The room I saw had an unappealing view of Kuhio Avenue with an earful of street noises, but the furnishings were adequate and the room comfortable. I don't recommend the $26 ground-floor rooms; for $29 double ($33 from December 20 to April 22) you can have quieter accommodations upstairs.

The exclusive high-rise hotels looming on either side of the **Hawaiian Colony** (1946 Ala Moana Boulevard; 941-3302) make it seem a comparatively small establishment. Actually it's an eighty-six-unit complex with laundry, sun deck, and pool. The rooms are a bit dark and rundown, but they do have air-conditioning. $22 double ($23.50 from December 20 to April 15).

Hawaii Dynasty Hotel (1830 Ala Moana Boulevard; 955-1111), just down the street, is easy walking distance from both Ala Moana Center and the beach. For the price, accommodations at this seventeen-story caravansary are relatively plush. Each room has air-conditioning, television, telephone, clock radio, carpeting, a shower-tub combination, and comfortable furnishings. The room I saw was quite spacious and contained a king-size bed. Standard accommodations are $25 single, $27 double (add $4 from December 20 until April 15).

Last (but not least) is the **Waikiki Grand Hotel** (134 Kapahulu Avenue; 923-1511), across the street from lush Kapiolani Park. The standard rooms (pegged at $30 double) are comfortable, pleasant places to park your bags. Downstairs there's a windswept lobby.

Waikiki Deluxe Hotels: Being a sentimentalist, my first choice among the deluxe facilities is Waikiki's premier hostelry, the **Moana Hotel** (2365 Kalakaua Avenue; 922-3111). Built in 1901, when Waikiki consisted only of thatch huts and woodframe houses scattered along a ribbon of sand, the Moana represents an integral part of Hawaii's history. And also being a traditionalist, I always ask for a room in the old section, where $39 double buys a night in nineteenth century Hawaii (or so it seems, surrounded by marbletop tables, brass beds, Victorian fruitwood chests, and overhead fans). If you seek modern convenience, book reservations in the hotel's new, air-conditioned section. Rooms here run upwards from $64. Other than the additions, and the fact that Sheraton presently runs this beachfront establishment, little is different from the days when Robert Louis Stevenson sat and wrote beneath the hotel's fabled banyan tree.

Another place Stevenson penned into eternity was Sans Souci Beach, just down the Waikiki strand. "If anyone," he stated, "desires such old-fashioned things as lovely scenery, quiet, pure air, clear sea water, good food, and heavenly sunsets hung out before his eyes over the Pacific...I recommend him cordially to Sans Souci." Of course, the roving Scotsman was writing before the **New Otani Kaimana Beach Hotel** (2863 Kalakaua Avenue; 923-1555) rose along the beach. But the place still maintains that reassuring air of repose that Stevenson always sought. Kapiolani Park and

Diamond Head backdrop the establishment, and the Otani is far enough from the center of Waikiki to escape the noise, but sufficiently close to catch the excitement. Two restaurants and an oceanside bar lend the feel of a big hotel, but with about 160 rooms the Otani manages to maintain a family atmosphere. And if that's not enough, it comes highly recommended by the Henriques clan, an old Jamaican family that knows its islands...and its hotels as well. Standard rooms are small, very nicely appointed, and priced from $40 double. Larger "ocean studio" accommodations overlooking the beach are $70 for two.

If you read the publicity brochures, **Park Shore Hotel** (110 Kapahulu Avenue; 923-0411) boasts that it represents "a special corner of Waikiki." And this 227-room hotel is indeed nicely situated, with graceful Kapiolani Park flanking one side and the blue Pacific another. It's an extremely attractive hotel, with lounge, restaurant, and shops downstairs, and eighteen stories of rooms above. The deluxe rooms, priced at $51 double ($58 from December through April), are spacious, pleasantly decorated accommodations overlooking the beach. Standard rooms ($35 and $40, respectively) are smaller and lack a view. My recommendation? Go deluxe.

It's an extra skip-and-a-hop to the beach from the nearby **Queen Kapiolani Hotel** (150 Kapahulu Avenue; 922-1941), which otherwise is an equally outstanding hotel. This 19-story facility shadows Diamond Head Crater and features a decorative theme reminiscent of royal Hawaii. The rooms are painted in soft hues and furnished with wicker furniture. During the slack season they price from $37 double; from December until March the cost is $43. A link in the Hawaiian Pacific Resorts chain, the Kapiolani contains a busy lobby and two restaurants at which you can dine freelance or on the American plan.

Holiday Inn Waikiki Beach (2570 Kalakaua Avenue; 922-2511) is a labyrinthine 25-story, 636-room facility in which I always get lost. Like Holiday Inns everywhere, it's pleasant, predictable, and popular. The room decor is unimaginative, but certainly acceptable. Rooms for two begin around $42. What can I say? It's the good old Holiday Inn, a common denominator for sure, but one that sums up pretty high.

If nothing else, the **Pacific Beach Hotel** (2490 Kalakaua Avenue; 922-1233) is aptly named. It happens to be right across the street from one of the most famous beaches in the entire Pacific. This facility also boasts the world's largest indoor oceanarium, a seafood restaurant guarded by an imposing statue of Neptune, another restaurant named Shogun, and the granddaddy of grand ballrooms. The rooms are spacious, pleasant (though undistinguished), and tagged from about $42 double ($48 from December to April). The last time I visited, the occupancy rate was hovering near 100 percent—and who's to argue with that? The place is kind of gimmicky, and decor in the public areas tends to high gauche, but it's a hotel with a lot of excitement.

Another hotel situated at the center of action is the **Waikiki Beachcomber** (2300 Kalakaua Avenue; 922-4646). Operated by Amfac Resorts Hawaii, which possesses a chain of reasonably priced Hawaiian hotels, the Beachcomber is set on the main drag of Waikiki just across the street from the beach. This high-rise hostelry contains a cluster of shops, plus several popular restaurants and lounges. There's also an ample lobby and a friendly ambience. Rooms, which begin at $41 double ($46 during peak season), are generally equipped with a refrigerator, color television, air-conditioner, and lanai. Despite its easygoing prices, the Beachcomber provides amenities usually found at highbrow hotels, including room service. I spent several days here during a recent Honolulu visit and definitely recommend the place.

Waikiki Ultra-Deluxe Hotels: The grande dame among Hawaii's grand hotels is the **Royal Hawaiian** (2259 Kalakaua Avenue; 923-7311). Next to the Moana, it's the oldest hotel in the islands: indeed, the "Pink Palace" has been a castle away from home since the 1920s. During the early days it was a special favorite of the steamer trunk set. Rockefellers and Fords honeymooned here, while such stars as Douglas Fairbanks and Mary Pickford checked in regularly. Today it's as elegant as ever, an ornate edifice painted shocking pink and resting defiantly among the steel-and-glass skyscrapers that have moved in down the block. The great lady's lobby is hung with chandeliers, the walkways are colonnaded, and the grounds impeccably landscaped. The only thing that seems changed are the hotel's many shops, which feature contemporary fashions and designs. Rooms in the old section are decorated with crystal light fixtures and period furniture; comfortable and charming affairs, they are priced from $74 double. In the Pink Palace's new tower, you'll trade a spot of sentiment for modern furnishings and an oceanfront lanai; $93 double.

If the Royal Hawaiian evokes the past, the **Hyatt Regency Waikiki** (2424 Kalakaua Avenue; 922-9292) represents Hawaii's future. The hotel's twin 40-story towers, rising across the street from Waikiki Beach, dominate the skyline. Separating these vaulting structures is a tiled courtyard encircled by shops, restaurants, and lounges. A two-and-a-half ton sculpture, reflective of Hawaiian mythology, overhangs the plaza; and, final touch, a spectacular waterfall tumbles several stories into a retaining pool lush with flowers and tropical plants. An architectural extravaganza, the Hyatt numbers among Hawaii's loveliest, most intriguing hotels. Standard rooms, which ably reveal the establishment's excellent taste in decor, range from $70 to $100 for oceanfront accommodations; oceanside suites are $175.

Another twin-tower facility overlooking Waikiki Beach is the **Hawaiian Regent Hotel** (2552 Kalakaua Avenue; 922-6611). This link in the Regent chain occupies over five acres of prime Honolulu real estate; with its marble-and-tile interior and open courtyard, the place certainly communicates a sense of spaciousness. There are four restaurants here (including the Third Floor, one of the city's finest), plus a championship tennis court and two pools. The entire affair, both within and without, is skillfully landscaped. The accommodations are as spacious and nicely appointed as the rest of the hotel. Standard rooms begin at $57 for two ($62 from December through March); one-bedroom suites run $200. If the room I stayed in (an oceanview facility tabbed at $79, or $84 during the peak season) is any indication, the Regent is worth the cost. The place was furnished with wicker chairs, a teak dresser-desk, and beds with woven *laubala* headboards, and included a mini-refrigerator. From the lanai I looked out upon the ocean and Diamond Head, and could even see a sliver of the distant Windward Coast. My appraisal: service was slightly sluggish, but otherwise the Regent is a top-rate hotel.

Waikiki's biggest, brashest and, by some accounts, best hotel is the **Sheraton-Waikiki Hotel** (2255 Kalakaua Avenue; 922-4422). Built in a curved wing design with both wings shadowing a sandy white beach, the Sheraton is simply overwhelming. The place lacks nothing: its myriad shops, restaurants, bars, and service centers give the impression of a self-contained city. One could easily spend a week in Waikiki journeying no further than the lobby and adjoining beach. For my taste, however, the Sheraton is a bit too overwhelming—there's too much glass and steel, too many crowds coursing through the grounds, and too little attention paid to too many things. But if you long to be located in action center, this is it, the very hub of Waikiki. If so, you'll find the rooms of moderate size, brightly decorated, and priced from $60 for a mountain view to $90 for oceanfront. And, for those willing to slum it at a first-class hotel, there are rooms in the Sheraton's manor wing for $39; they lack a view and a lanai, and are rather small, but should prove adequate.

Away from these other hotels, and apart from the commotion of central Waikiki, is the **Colony Surf Hotel** (2895 Kalakaua Avenue; 923-5751). Set comfortably in the saddle between Diamond Head and the Pacific, this beachfront establishment is Hawaii's bid for a "hidden" resort of world-class status. It's a hotel for discriminating guests who want to feel at home while away, a place sufficiently removed to provide the seclusion which celebrities and canny vacationers seek. Matter of fact, the Colony Surf is proof that the local limelight is really at the periphery of Waikiki's brilliantly lit center: Richard Pryor checks in regularly, and during a recent visit I discovered Lana Turner on the guest list. In addition to the solitude, these stars come for the accommodations, which are nothing less than opulent. The rooms are elegantly appointed with rattan furnishings, plush carpets, mirrored walls, and graceful potted plants, and feature fully-equipped kitchenettes. They begin at $90 nightly for two; if you book one of the more expensive units, you'll find one wall built entirely of shutters which open on to the ocean. Or, if money really is an object after all, you might consider a $65-a-night studio in the **Colony East Hotel**, a little sister establishment next door.

Another of Honolulu's more prestigious hotels sits several miles outside Waikiki in the city's elite Kahala district. With a white-sand beach, seaside pool, and a waterfall cascading through its luxurious grounds, the **Kahala Hilton** (5000 Kahala Avenue; 734-2211) is an enchanting environment. The grounds are landscaped with a variety of palm trees, as well as bougainvillea and other flowering plants; an exotic lagoon is filled with dolphins, penguins, sea turtles, and multihued tropical fish. Once inside, the lobby's high-ceilinged rooms and Italian glass chandeliers reflect the stature of this 370 room hotel. The private rooms are equally outstanding. Occupying about 600 square feet of space, they are possibly the largest hotel rooms you'll encounter. Their parquet floors and fastidious decor will doubtless number them among the most fashionable as well. In price, rooms vary from $95 to $200, depending on floor level and proximity to the ocean; suites climb from $200 for a "junior" to $690 for a top-class two-bedroom accommodation. I've always thought the Kahala a bit too formal; the dress code and refined air seem more appropriate to the mainland than the islands. But for service and style it has to be regarded as one of Hawaii's premier hotels.

GREATER HONOLULU HOTELS

Dotted around Honolulu are a handful of other hotels. These range in price from budget to moderate to deluxe, and can generally be depended upon for cleanliness, service, and local color. If you're conducting business in the city or just want a room away from the bustling world of Waikiki, you might consider reserving accommodations in one of the following.

There are two very inexpensive places near the University of Hawaii's Manoa campus. Located a mile from Waikiki, they're a short bus ride or brisk walk from the beach. The first, **Atherton Branch YMCA** (1810 University Avenue; 946-0253), provides accomodations similar to the Y's central branch in Waikiki. The Atherton Branch, however, is a co-ed operation. There are no athletic facilities. Rooms are $9.50 single, $14 double (plus a $5 membership fee). Students have first priority, so rooms are often difficult to obtain. Three-day minimum stay. Sorry, no reservations.

Second is the nearby **Hale Aloha Youth Hostel** (2323 Sea View Avenue; 946-0591), a dormitory-style crash pad with separate living quarters for men and women. Kitchen facilities are available. $4.50 per night, plus a $14 membership fee.

There are also two YMCAs in downtown Honolulu. **Armed Services YMCA** (250 South Hotel Street; 524-5600) has ample athletic facilities and will house men, women, and children. (A day-care center is available.) Rates are $12 single, $14.50 double, for a room with shared bath. The **Nuuanu YMCA** (1441 Pali Highway; 536-3556) also has complete recreational facilities, but permits men only. Single rooms here rent for $11 ($13 with private bath) and doubles are $18.

Centrally located between Waikiki and downtown Honolulu is the **Nakamura Hotel** (1140 South King Street; 537-1951). It's a pleasant place, but the only reason I can conceive for staying here is the locale. The hotel itself is adequate; the rooms are neatly furnished, carpeted, and equipped with air-conditioning and telephones. I'd ask for accommodations on the *mauka* side, since the other side fronts noisy King Street.

Farther downtown, on the outskirts of Chinatown, is the **Kobayashi Hotel** (250 North Beretania Street; 536-2377). This is an excellent spot to capture the local color of Honolulu's Chinese section, though the hotel itself is rather nondescript. The rooms are clean but uncarpeted, sparsely furnished, and practically devoid of decoration. They rent for $20 double ($23 with a kitchenette).

In the deluxe hotel category are two facilities on the outskirts of Waikiki. The first, **Pagoda Hotel** (1525 Rycroft Street; 941-6611), is sufficiently removed from the crowded enclave but still within striking distance of the beach and the district's shopping centers. Known particularly for its "floating" restaurant, this hotel is an especially good choice for families. There are swimming pools for both children and adults, and a friendly ambience that adds to the pleasure of traveling with kids. The accommodations are very roomy, furnished in a plain but comfortable fashion, and equipped with telephone, television, air-conditioner, and wall-to-wall carpeting. Most rooms offer a view of the hotel's garden or the distant mountains, and are priced from $30 to $38 double (add $3 for a kitchenette). The hotel's adjoining **Pagoda Terrace** offers family rates: a two-bedroom facility housing as many as six people for $44 nightly.

The other deluxe hostelry is a place called the **Ala Moana Hotel** (410 Atkinson Drive; 955-4811), located next to Ala Moana Center, Hawaii's largest shopping complex. This 36-floor, 1,200-room hotel is also situated just a few blocks from a picturesque beach. Clearly the key word here is access: in addition to its immediate surroundings, the Ala Moana itself features numerous shops and restaurants, plus several lounges renowned for their local entertainers. All this combined with a friendly staff and a grandly decorated lobby, make it an excellent selection among Honolulu hotels. The small "minimum"-class rooms run $48 double, when available.

"Superior" rooms, which are ingeniously appointed and decorated with sketches of Hawaiian scenes, are $78 for two; the "deluxe" facilities, with ocean view, are $88.

Restaurants

Hawaii's cuisine is as diverse as its population, and nowhere in the islands will you find such a variety of restaurants as in Honolulu. Waikiki alone seems like the United Nations' answer to good dining. Look around and you'll encounter American, Hawaiian, Chinese, Japanese, Italian, French, Thai, and Mexican restaurants, plus dining spots representing numerous other national cuisines.

To facilitate your search through this international maze, I've divided the listings into restaurants located in Waikiki and those in the Greater Honolulu area. The Waikiki establishments have been further divided into cost categories: budget, moderate, deluxe, and ultra-deluxe. Regardless of personal taste, or the size of your purse, you'll find good kitchens galore.

WAIKIKI RESTAURANTS

Waikiki Budget Restaurants: For a culinary adventure Hawaiian style, you'll have to cross the Ala Wai Canal to **Ono Hawaiian Food** (726 Kapahulu Avenue; 737-2275). This informal cafe (the walls are covered with autographed photos of local performers) serves delicious Hawaiian food at *kanaka* prices. There are several specialties including a *lau lau* plate with *lomi* salmon and *poi*, plus a la carte dishes like *opihi* (limpets), *kalua* pig, squid, dried *aku* (a local fish), and many more. I lunched here recently and found myself the only *haole* in one very crowded cafe. Highly recommended.

Seven Star Chinese Restaurant (2260 Kuhio Avenue; 923-5828) is tucked away in an alley off bustling Kuhio Avenue, but it's another eatery you shouldn't miss. The restaurant may be tiny, but the menu is huge, listing over fifty fish, fowl, beef, pork, and vegetable dishes, all priced around $3 to $5. They even have Chinese-style crepes with Asian dishes such as beef broccoli rolled into a pancake.

Peking Garden (307 Royal Hawaiian Avenue; 922-3401), a small stand with several sidewalk tables, is another prime choice. This walk-up cafe serves both Chinese and Japanese meals. I especially enjoyed the *shoyu* chicken with rice and spicy *kim chi* salad. The tab for this or any of the pork cutlet, teriyaki, and other dishes was only about $3. Best recommendation of all: it's frequented primarily by Asians.

Petite Tokyo, a tiny lunch counter on Liliuokalani Avenue just a few doors in from Kalakaua, also draws an Asian crowd. Serving *udon*, teriyaki, and curry dishes for about $3, it's a great spot for snacks.

Another likely place is **Sandwich House Gourmet** (2526 Kalakaua Avenue; 923-0804). It may well be the only place in Hawaii serving sukiyaki on toast or teriyaki roast beef sandwiches. American sandwiches too.

But my favorite Japanese budget restaurant is **Irifune** (563 Kapahulu Avenue; 737-1141), a charming sit-down restaurant with a warm and friendly ambience. Most of the tasty sukiyaki, curry, teriyaki, and tempura dishes are priced from $4 to $5. And, to add elegance without expense, you can bring your own *sake*.

For meals on the cheap, there's nothing this side of Asia to beat **Minute Chef** (120 Kaiulani Avenue; 922-5811). Granted the decor is neo-naugahyde and the walls seem to glow, but with dinner entrees from $3 and breakfasts even lower, who's arguing? American cuisine; good bet for a square meal.

For just a tad more you can dine overlooking the water at **Waikiki Circle Restaurant** (2464 Kalakaua Avenue; 923-1571). Located just off Waikiki Beach, this hotel facility features such exotic dishes as shrimp tempura and *mahimahi*, plus standard fare—chops, chicken, and steak. With entrees priced around $5 and that blue Pacific right out there, it's hard to beat. Also open for breakfast and lunch.

The **Surf Restaurant** (2496 Kalakaua Avenue; 923-3638) also has a conveniently priced breakfast, lunch, and dinner menu. Yet another member of the naugahyde school of interior design, the Surf nonetheless contains a South Seas decor that renders it a pleasant place to dine. The cafe's location across from Waikiki Beach makes it convenient for hungry sunlovers. The cuisine is All-American—hamburgers, hot and cold sandwiches, fried chicken, etc.

Eggs and Things (436 Ena Row; 949-0820), a little hole in the Waikiki wall, offers the best deal in bargain basement breakfasts. Open from 11 at night until 2 o'clock the next afternoon, it features an eggs-and-pancakes special for about a buck; an assortment of waffle and crepe dishes is also available.

Another popular spot is **Hamburger Mary's Organic Grill** (2109 Kuhio Avenue; 922-6722), a sidewalk cafe fringed with potted plants. The adjoining bar is gay, but Mary's organic-panic sandwiches attract gays and straights alike. You can pull up a producer's chair, kick back in the sunshine, and order a plain Hamburger Mary, a salsa-smothered Hamburger Maria, or any of several vegetarian sandwiches. All are tagged between $4 and $5, and served on wheat grain bread. There's also a concoct-your-own omelette: just add avocado, shrimp, sprouts, pineapple, cheese, or several other goodies.

If you're willing to go Mediterranean, try **It's Greek To Me** (2201 Kalakaua Avenue; 922-2733). Located in the Royal Hawaiian Center, it features falafels, *spanakopita*, and *hummos*, plus some delicious Greek desserts. Open for lunch and dinner, it's a great place to snack.

At the International Market Place's **Colonial House Cafeteria** (2330 Kalakaua Avenue; 923-7434) you can dine out on the lanai and watch the crowds passing under the banyan tree. With wooden shutters, brick partitions, and white pillars, this bustling restaurant has a vague aura of Hawaii's bygone colonial days. The $3 price tag on most hot meals is a welcome anachronism too.

Waikiki Moderately Priced Restaurants: Best bets in this category are the buffets. At the **Parrot House Restaurant**, located in the Hotel Miramar (2345 Kuhio Avenue; 922-2077), you'll find a nightly buffet that provides all you can eat for around $6. There's also an a la carte menu with fish, veal, chicken, and steak dishes priced between $6 to $10. The restaurant also offers a varied breakfast and lunch menu. Check it out; the hotel lobby alone is a feast for the eyes.

Perry's Smorgasbord, with its two locations—at the Outrigger Hotel (2335 Kalakaua Avenue; 923-0711, ext. 48) and the Coral Seas Hotel (250 Lewers; 923-3881)—have a less expensive buffet at dinner, lunch, and breakfast. With an extensive salad bar, plus a host of meat and fish dishes, this all-you-can-eat emporium is hard to beat. I'd suggest the Outrigger branch; it's right on the waterfront.

HOW TO BEAT THE HEAT WITH A SWEET TREAT

Since the early days of Hawaiian royalty, people have complained about Honolulu's shirt-sticking weather. Come summer, temperatures rise and the trade winds stop blowing. Visitors seeking a golden tan discover they're baking without browning. And residents begin to think that their city, renowned as a cultural melting pot, is actually a pressure cooker.

With the ocean all around, relief is never far away. But a lot of folks, when not heading for the beaches, have found another way to cool off. Shave ice. Known as ice frappes among the Japanese originators and snow cones back on the mainland, these frozen treats are Hawaii's answer to the Good Humor man.

They're made with ice that's been shaved from a block into thin slivers, packed into a cone-shaped cup, and covered with sweet syrup. Health-minded people eat the ice plain, and some folks ask for a scoop of ice cream or sweet black beans underneath the shavings. Most people just order it with their favorite syrup flavors—grape, root beer, cola, cherry, orange, lemon-lime, vanilla, fruit punch, banana, strawberry or whatever.

Whichever you choose, you'll find it only costs about half a buck at the many stands sprinkled around town. Near Waikiki, you might try **Wiki Wiki Coffee House** in Ala Moana Center (1450 Ala Moana Boulevard). **Shiihara Store** (525 Kapahulu), or **Goodie Goodie Drive Inn** (946 Coolidge). Watch for stands up on the North Shore, too. No doubt you'll see a long line outside Oahu's most famous shave ice store, **Matsumoto's** (66-087 Kam Highway in Haleiwa).

As a matter of fact, any place where the sun blazes overhead you're liable to find someone trying to beat the heat by slurping up a "snow cone" before it melts into mush.

For Japanese food, my vote goes to **Shirahama** (2166 Kalakaua Avenue; 923-8156). This comfortable little cafe has booths and a counter across which you can watch the chef prepare your meal. There's an extensive dinner menu with tempura, *misoyaki,* sukiyaki, and teriyaki dishes priced around $6. The lunch menu is almost identical, though lower-priced.

At the **Cock's Roost** (2330 Kalakaua Avenue; 923-3229), you can dine on a wrought-iron patio overlooking the International Market Place. Dinners at this spiffy establishment run around $9 and include beef kakob, *mahimahi,* broiled chicken, and sirloin. There's also a $3 sandwich menu in the afternoon.

The Noodle Shop (2375 Ala Wai Boulevard; 922-4744), a unique restaurant in the Waikiki Sand Villa Hotel, features a wide variety of meals, all prepared with a common ingredient—noodles. There's spaghetti, beef stroganoff, fettuccine, sukiyaki, *udon* (Oriental noodles cooked in sukiyaki sauce), *pansit* (the same noodles prepared with ham, bamboo shoots, onions, and other vegetables), and, of course, *saimin*. All these meals are set comfortably in the $7 neighborhood and include a visit to the salad bar. There's an additional menu for the anti-noodle contingent, plus soups, salads, and plate lunches.

One way to add several other moderately priced restaurants to your list is by considering the **Jolly Roger** chain (located at 150 Kaiulani Avenue; 923-2172; at 2244 Kalakaua Avenue; 923-1885; and in various locations outside Waikiki). Each link is done up in nautical style to fit a buccaneer theme. Possibly the friendliest pirates you'll ever encounter, the folks at Jolly Roger serve standard American fare, plus a few local favorites such as *mahimahi* and teriyaki steak. Considering they're buccaneers, they don't take much at all: entrees are priced around $7.

Waikiki Deluxe Restaurants: **Canlis Restaurant** (2100 Kalakaua Avenue; 923-2324), in the islands since 1947, comes well-recommended by several gourmet friends. With its high-beamed ceiling and smoky ambience, Canlis is a prime place for a relaxed meal. A la carte selections generally vary from $11 to $19 and include Canlis specialties such as Parisian-style crab legs and teriyaki steak strips. The other surf-and-turf plates are just as mouth-watering: salmon, lobster, oysters, shish kebab, filet mignon, or baby squab. This intimate establishment is part of a restaurant chain with branches in San Francisco, Seattle, and Portland.

Poolside at the Waikikian Hotel, you'll find **Tahitian Lanai** (1811 Ala Moana Boulevard; 946-6541). Here you can dine overlooking a lagoon or hide away in back at one of the restaurant's canopied tables. Regardless of your location, you'll find that the Lanai's bold woodcarvings, exotic totem poles, and flowering gardens exude an aura of Polynesia. The dinner menu reflects these surroundings: there's a Hawaiian dinner with *poi, kalua* pig, and *lomi* salmon, plus other island dishes such as *mahimahi* and shrimp curry. For the less adventurous, the menu includes steak and chicken. Entrees cost around $10; in addition to breakfast, lunch, and dinner, the restaurant also features a Sunday brunch.

With branches spreading all across Honolulu, **Furusato** has become synonymous with fine Japanese dining. The original restaurant (134 Kapahulu Avenue; 923-8878), a Honolulu landmark, maintains the tranquil ambience and outstanding cuisine for which the company is renowned. Overlooking luxurious Kapiolani Park, Furusato has a lunch buffet featuring *sushi, sashimi*, and other Asian specialties. During dinner hours you'll find an array of Japanese dishes—tempura plates with shrimp, crab, scallop, or even sea eel and squid; a brothy serving of *shabu shabu* including sliced beef and assorted vegetables; standard sukiyaki and *sashimi* dishes; and, for the multicultural gourmet, Maine lobster prepared a la Japan. Dinner entrees are $10 to $25, the lunch buffet about $5.

For *teppanyaki* style cooking, my choice is **Kobe Japanese Steak House** (1841 Ala Moana Boulevard; 941-4444). Here master chefs prepare the meal at your table, handling their cutting knives with the aplomb of showmen. Adding to the atmosphere, the restaurant is decorated Japanese-fashion with paper screens, painted scrolls, and a carp pool. There are steak, lobster, scallop, and chicken dishes, varying between $12 and $18, all prepared on tableside grills. For a culinary insight into Hawaii's Asian culture, this soft-lit retreat is a natural.

Nick's Fishmarket (2070 Kalakaua Avenue; 955-6333), rest assured, is much more refined than its name. The dim lighting, private booths, and congenial staff make it one of Waikiki's best seafood restaurants. In addition to island fish dishes there are numerous mainland catches; the shellfish selections include abalone, soft shell crab, lobster, and prawns. If popularity is any indication of quality, this fishmarket is tops. As the cartoon decorating one wall says, "You know something about Nick's? If it weren't full every night, more people would come here."

Another poshly appointed restaurant is **Spat's** (2424 Kalakaua Avenue; 922-9292). With stained-glass windows, brass-and-oak bars, stuffed armchairs, and soft lighting, the place recreates a speakeasy atmosphere. Appropriately, Spat's is downstairs from the equally elegant Hyatt Regency Waikiki. With dinners tabbed around $12, this "family style" Italian restaurant offers Mediterranean-style seafood, lamb, and chicken dishes. For the daring, there is a selection of pastas and antipastos.

You can judge for yourself whether **Bobby McGee's Conglomeration** (2885 Kalakaua Avenue; 922-1282) is the best place to eat in Waikiki; it's definitely the wackiest. First there's the interior—call it neo-Baroque (or perhaps high gauche)—gilded mirrors, wood stoves, chandeliers, ceiling fans, and an old bathtub that serves as a salad bar. Then there are the waiters and waitresses, each in a different costume—Indian, dancehall girl, caballero, magician, referee—and each playing the part. Though your waiter, dressed as a serf, may start speaking in Russian, you'll find the menu is in English. Further, the dishes are more familiar than the bizarre surroundings: steak, chops, seafood, fowl, and, of course, that salad bar in the bathtub; dinners around $10 or $15.

Waikiki Ultra-Deluxe Restaurants: For high dining I like **Michel's** (Colony Surf Hotel, 2895 Kalakaua Avenue; 923-6552), a white-tablecloth French restaurant replete with chandeliers, statuettes, and oil paintings. The lovely ocean view highlights an haute cuisine atmosphere. The a la carte menu generally ranges between $14 and $24. Michel serves a few beef dishes and a wealth of seafood selections, including lobster, a surf platter with shrimp, lobster and crab, and a similar dish, Coquille Saint Jacques a la Rainee, cooked with saffron and Pernod. Then, of course, there are tournedos, veal *medaillons,* filet mignon, chateaubriand, and so on. For the ultimate in elegance try Michel's, but remember your dinner jackets, please.

The lights are dim and the mood amber at the Hawaiian Regent Hotel on **The Third Floor** (2552 Kalakaua Avenue; 922-6611). This gourmet restaurant is set in a spectacular room decorated with torches and colorful banners and topped with a vaulted ceiling. The high-backed chairs combine privacy with comfort; the menu varies nightly. Among the frequent delicacies are rack of lamb, veal *medaillons*, duck a l'orange, and chateaubriand; there's also an appetizer bar with numerous finger-size treats. Entrees reside in the $20 neighborhood. As to quality, The Third Floor seems to win a coveted *Travel/Holiday Magazine* award almost every year.

The soft strains of a classical guitar, indoor plants strung with lights, red plush furniture, art works placed modestly along the walls—all add to the ambience at **Bagwell's 2424** (2424 Kalakaua Avenue; 922-9292). The menu at this Hyatt Regency Waikiki restaurant features a Continental selection ranging from tenderloin with truffle sauce to local fish served with watercress and ginger. Entrees are about $20, and the list of California and French wines is among the finest in the islands. Though many consider it Hawaii's number one restaurant, Bagwell's disappointed me when I dined here recently. The entrees simply weren't distinguished enough to warrant the price, though the service was impeccable and the souffles otherworldly.

The experience of dining at **Champeaux's** (1164 Ala Moana Boulevard; 949-3811) begins even before you reach the restaurant. Thirty stories before, as a matter of fact, as soon as you step onto the elevator that climbs the side of the Ilikai Hotel. With a yacht basin, park, and the entire coastline falling away below, this glass enclosure whisks you to a top-of-the-skyscraper restaurant. In addition to the extraordinary view, Champeaux's features a nouvelle cuisine menu. Both island and imported fish are prepared in this European fashion; for instance you can order poached salmon with lobster sauce or lobster flamed with cognac. Other dishes include rack of lamb, duckling glazed with brandy, pheasant, filet mignon, and veal prepared with papaya and curry. A la carte dishes will set you back $15 to $20, and the Sunday champagne brunch is $10.

Several miles outside Waikiki, at the elite Kahala Hilton, there is an haute cuisine establishment, **Maile Restaurant** (5000 Kahala Avenue; 734-2211), that compares favorably with any you'll find. Here you can settle into a soft armchair and order from a kimono-clad waitress. With orchids and potted plants all about, sconces, chandeliers, lace tablecloths, and an interior fountain, the atmosphere is subdued and graceful. The menu is equally impressive. Even the appetizers are gourmet selections—smoked salmon, Alaskan king crab, escargots, and oysters florentine. Main courses, not to be outdone, include veal *medaillons*, trout fillet, chateaubriand, roast duckling island-style (prepared with bananas, lichees, mandarin oranges, and peaches, then flamed with Grand Marnier), rack of lamb, lobster tail, scallops *meuniere*, and on and on and on. The menu is prix fixe ($30.50 covers everything except tax and tip), and dinner jackets are de rigueur.

GREATER HONOLULU RESTAURANTS

Rather than list the city's restaurants according to price, I'll group them by area. As you get away from Waikiki you'll be dining with a more local crowd and tasting foods more representative of island cuisine. So I would certainly advise checking out some of Greater Honolulu's eating places.

Right next to Waikiki, in Ala Moana Center (1450 Ala Moana), there are several good restaurants. Best of all is **Patti's Chinese Kitchen** (946-5002), a crowded and noisy cafeteria. For about $2 you can choose two main dishes plus a side order of fried rice, chop suey, or *chow fun*. The courses include almond duck, lemon sauce chicken, tofu, beef tomato, sweet-and-sour pork, barbecued ribs, pig's feet, and shrimp with vegetables. For under $3 you can choose four dishes. It's quite simply the best place near Waikiki for a low-cost meal.

There's also the **Poi Bowl**, with both a take-out stand and sit-down restaurant serving Hawaiian dishes, and **Lyn's Delicatessen** (941-3388), featuring a full line of deli sandwiches as well as chicken baskets and plate lunches.

For health foods, try **The Haven** (947-8040), a largely vegetarian cafe. The many varieties of natural sandwiches are served on wheat-grain bread with lettuce, tomato, and sprouts. They include asparagus tip, pineapple, and cream cheese concoctions, plus several more creative sandwiches fashioned from traditional fixings like ham, salami, barbecued beef, and cheese. There are also salads, juices, and smoothies. All moderately priced.

China House (1349 Kapiolani Boulevard; 949-6622), right next to Ala Moana Center, consists of one large room. Nevertheless, its high ceiling, wood paneling, and Asian mural make it an appealing place to enjoy a Cantonese meal. At lunch you can order individual appetizer-size portions, *dim sum* style. During both lunch and dinner there is a 113-item menu. Within this catalog of meals are soups, including shark's fin and bird nest; meat entrees, such as shredded beef in taro and bitter lemon pork; fowl dishes, for instance lemon chicken or stuffed duck (not to mention duck webs with oyster sauce); and a school of fish entrees. Most selections are priced comfortably in the $5 to $7 bracket.

For another taste of the Orient, try **Pagoda Floating Restaurant** (1525 Rycroft Street; 941-6611). This entire restaurant-in-the-round is built above a pond filled with gaily colored *koi* fish. A fountain and several waterfalls feed the pond, and the surrounding grounds are skillfully landscaped. The restaurant that "floats" within this environment is a two-tiered affair featuring a separate dining room on either level. The Lotus Room upstairs offers Japanese cuisine, while the lower Koi Dining Room prepares island seafood dishes. Entrees at both average about $11, and at lunch you'll get by with $7 or so.

An excellent choice at the University of Hawaii Manoa campus is the **International Garden Court Restaurant**, an attractive cafeteria at the University's East-West Center. Located in Jefferson Hall, the spacious dining area looks out on a waterfall and Japanese garden. It's an excellent place to meet students from all over the world while sampling an international cuisine.

Off campus you might be interested in the pizza, hero sandwiches, spaghetti, or salad bar at **Mama Mia** (in Puck's Alley, 1015 University Avenue; 547-5233). Open for lunch and dinner, it's a great place to snack or stop for a cold beer.

For health foods, **Down To Earth Natural Foods** (2525 South King Street; 947-7678) and **Vim and Vigor** (in Puck's Alley, 1015 University Avenue; 947-5700) both have snack bars in their stores.

Or you can check out **Anna Banana's** (2440 South Beretania Street; 946-5190), a combination bar and Mexican restaurant that draws a swinging crowd. Located a half-mile from campus, this dim eatery serves burritos, enchiladas, and other south-o'-the-border favorites. Decorated in slapdash fashion with propellers, antlers, boxing gloves, and trophies, Anna's is the local center for slumming.

By contrast, to enter **The Willows** nearby (901 Hausten Street; 946-4808) is to walk through a tropical garden into a Polynesian setting. The flowering trees and thatch-shaded tables are reminiscent of old Hawaii. There's a carp pond adding to the ambience, plus a menu featuring fine Hawaiian and seafood dishes. The restaurant, its staff insists, is dedicated to "the very best that nature and Hawaii provide." Here nature provides such bounties as sauteed scallops, scampi, and a traditional *poi* dinner (with island favorites like *laulau* and *lomi* salmon). Dinner selections price around $13, lunch about $8. The Willows quite simply is a must for anyone wishing to combine good dining with a Polynesian experience.

There are five dining spots located midway between Waikiki and downtown Honolulu which I particularly like. The first is **Laulima** (2239 South King Street; 947-3844), possibly Honolulu's finest vegetarian restaurant. Here, in mellow surroundings, you can relax on floor mats or handcrafted chairs. The daytime menu features such salad innovations as an Avocado Island set in a sea of greens and a Tomato Volcano with a craterful of guacamole, plus a varied sandwich selection. For dinner, a specially prepared meal is served every night, with soup, salad, bread, and tea.

Also on South King Street sits one of Honolulu's best moderately priced Chinese restaurants. The decor at **King Tsin Restaurant** (1486 South King Street; 946-3273) is rather bland, but the Mandarin cuisine adds plenty of spice. You can order Szechuan dishes like shredded pork or a Mongolian beef dish. These are plenty hot; you might want to try the milder seafood, pork, vegetable, fowl, and beef dishes.

For Southeast Asian cuisine, try **Thai House** (1254 South King Street; 521-1606). At this modest cafe you can savor *kang som* (hot-and-sour fish soup), fried pork with garlic and pepper, or mustard green cabbage. Or check out the **Vietnam Restaurant** (828-D Dreier Street; 533-3194). With a list of delicious dishes priced around $4 or $5, it's the perfect hideaway. Sample items like *chao tom* (grilled shrimp cake on sugar cane), *bo nhung dam* (vinegar beef), *thit ga ca ri* (coconut chicken curry), and *banh xeo* (crepe stuffed with bean sprouts).

Honolulu has several fine seafood restaurants. Some of them, fittingly enough, are located right on the water. But for an authentic seafront feel, it's nice to be where the fishing boats actually come in. **Fisherman's Wharf** (1009 Ala Moana Boulevard; 538-3808) provides just such an atmosphere. Boasting "two decks of superb dining," this sprawling facility is festooned with nautical gear. The "Captain's Bridge" topside has a shoalful of seafood selections ranging from broiled salmon to Alaskan king crab, and varying in price from $8 to $18.

In downtown Honolulu, near the city's financial center, are two modest cafes which I particularly like. One, **People's Cafe** (1310 Pali Highway; 536-5789), has been serving Hawaiian food for forty years. The place is owned by a Japanese family, which helps explain the teriyaki dishes on the menu. But primarily the food is Polynesian: this is a splendid spot to order *poi, lomi* salmon, *kalua* pig, and other island favorites. *Ono, ono!*

The **Tasty Broiler** (corner of Nimitz Highway and Smith Street; 533-3329) is my other haunt. It ain't much on atmosphere — just a couple of counters with swivel seats, some tables, and chairs. But it's the only place I've been where you can get a lobster tail dinner for $9, and Alaskan king crab and steak for about $8, plus other, more pedestrian plates at plebian prices.

Another good seafood spot is the nearby **Merchant Square Oyster Bar** (923 Nuuanu Avenue; 523-7906). Much more intimate than the Tasty Broiler, this dimly lighted nook serves oysters on the half-shell, clam chowder, seafood cocktails, and salads. There are also numerous entrees, comfortably tabbed between $6 and $7, including seafood quiche, deviled crab with artichoke, scallops au gratin, shrimp curry, and steamed clams.

For Chinese food, try **Yong Sing Restaurant** (1055 Alakea Street; 531-1367).This high-ceilinged establishment, catering to local businesspeople, has some delicious dishes. I thought the oyster sauce chicken particularly tasty. With its daily lunch specials, Yong Sing is a perfect stopoff when you're shopping or sightseeing downtown.

But for the true flavor of China, head over to Chinatown, just a few blocks from downtown Honolulu. Amid the tumbledown buildings and jumble of shops, there's one restaurant you must not miss — **Wo Fat** (115 North Hotel Street; 533-6393). Operating for over ninety years, this is the area's oldest

eating place, an institution in itself. If you don't eat here, at least tour the place. This cavernous establishment contains three floors and a knockout decor. The second-story, where I'd recommend dining, is painted from pillar to ceiling with dragons and ornate Asian designs. Add Chinese lanterns, brush paintings, and a mural, and you have an extravagant display of Chinese art. The cuisine, too, is varied: you'll have to go to Hong Kong for a wider choice of delicious Cantonese dishes. There are hundreds of pork, beef, duck, seafood and chicken dishes, plus old standbys like won ton, chop suey, and chow mein. All are generally priced around $4 a dish.

Fat Siu Lau (100 North Beretania Street; 538-7081), another imposing establishment, in the Cultural Plaza, is highly recommended by local gourmet Malcolm Tyau. This gilt-edged eatery also offers a Cantonese cuisine with dishes tabbed around $4.

LUAUS AND DINNER SHOWS

Events such as these, combining dinner with an evening of entertainment, are listed in the "Nightlife" section below.

Grocery Markets

During your Hawaiian visit, the best way to hold the budget on food bills is by preparing some meals yourself. If your hotel or condominium accommodation includes a kitchenette, you can cook up a storm. Otherwise, it's always easy to make sandwiches or pack a picnic. The best places to find the fixings for these homemade meals are the supermarkets in the Greater Honolulu area. They are competitive in price, and stocked with seemingly everything a hungry vacationer's heart (and stomach!) could desire. Waikiki also has a few shops; though they may be closer to where you are staying, generally their prices will be higher and their stock lower.

WAIKIKI GROCERY STORES

There are two moderate-sized supermarkets in Waikiki. Both the **Fast Stop Food Market** (Discovery Bay Shopping Center, 1778 Ala Moana Boulevard) and **The Food Pantry** (2370 Kuhio Avenue) are inflated in price, but conveniently located. The former is open 8 a.m. to 10 p.m. Monday through

Saturday and 8 a.m. to 8 p.m. Sunday; the latter is open from 8 a.m. until 11 p.m. daily.

ABC Discount Stores, a chain of sundry shops with branches all around Waikiki, are also convenient, but have a very limited stock and even higher prices.

There is another grocery store on the outskirts of Waikiki that can be easily reached by car or bus. It's a sprawling supermarket called **Foodland**, situated in the Ala Moana Center (1450 Ala Moana Boulevard). You should find everything you need here, at prices below the Waikiki groceries; but keep in mind that the Greater Honolulu stores are cheaper yet.

WAIKIKI HEALTH FOOD STORES

Vim and Vigor has a standard stock of natural food items in its stores at 437 Kapahulu Avenue and in Ala Moana Center (1450 Ala Moana Boulevard).

GREATER HONOLULU GROCERY STORES

The best place to shop near the University of Hawaii's Manoa campus is at **Star Market**, 2470 South King Street. It's a large supermarket, open from 8:30 a.m. to 10 p.m. Monday through Saturday, and on Sunday from 8:30 a.m. to 8 p.m.

Midway between Waikiki and downtown Honolulu there's a **Times Super Market** at 1290 South Beretania, and a **Safeway** at 1121 South Beretania. There's another **Safeway** in downtown Honolulu at 1360 Pali Highway. All are spacious, amply stocked, price-competitive, bland supermarkets.

You might want to browse around the mom 'n' pop grocery stores spotted throughout Chinatown. They're marvelous places to pick up Chinese foodstuffs and to capture local color.

GREATER HONOLULU HEALTH FOOD STORES

The best place in Honolulu to buy health foods is at **Down To Earth Natural Foods** (2525 South King Street) near the University of Hawaii's Manoa campus. **Kokua Country Foods**, a cooperative market nearby at 2357 South Beretania, is another excellent choice.

In downtown Honolulu, look for **The Nutrition Center** (700 Bishop Street). This shop contains a limited assortment of items for the health-minded and diet-conscious shoppers.

GREATER HONOLULU SPECIALTY SHOPS

Don't miss the **Open Market** at the Cultural Plaza (corner of Beretania and Mauna Kea) in Chinatown. It's a great place to shop for fresh foods. There are numerous stands selling fish, produce, poultry, meat, baked goods, and island fruits, all at low-overhead prices.

Shopping

Honolulu is *the* place to shop in all Hawaii. This city by the sea not only supports over half Hawaii's populace, but most of its stores and businesses as well. Honolulu is the only large metropolitan area within a 2,000-mile radius, so whatever merchandise you seek can most likely be found here.

WAIKIKI

This bustling enclave is a veritable mecca for shoppers. Browsing the countless shops is like studying a catalog of Hawaiian handicrafts. Everything is here; and you'll find a few bargains besides. Next to suntanning and surfing, shopping is Waikiki's most popular sport.

For budget shoppers, one place I particularly recommend is **Duke's Lane**. This alleyway, running from Kalakaua to Kuhio near the International Market Place, may be the best place in all Hawaii to buy coral and jade jewelry. Either side of the Lane is flanked by mobile stands selling rings, necklaces, earrings, stick pins, bracelets, etc. It's a prime place to barter for tiger eyes, opals, and mother-of-pearl pieces.

The main shopping scene is in the malls. **Waikiki Shopping Plaza** (2270 Kalakaua Avenue) has six floors of stores and restaurants. Here are jewelers, sundries, and boutiques, plus specialty shops like **Waldenbooks** (922-4154), with an excellent line of paperbacks as well as bestsellers; **Asia Arts and Furniture** (922-2655); and a quaint little place called **Ling's Things** (923-2583). All the shops in this unique complex are built around a 75-foot indoor fountain.

Following a somewhat different theme is **King's Alley** (on Kaiulani between Kalakaua and Kuhio), designed as a Victorian village. Here over 40 shops surround several courtyards.

International Market Place (2330 Kalakaua Avenue) is my favorite browsing place. With tiny shops and vending stands spotted around the sprawling grounds, it's a marvelous shopping complex. There's an old banyan spreading across the market, plus thatched treehouses, a carp pond, brick sidewalks, and woodfront stores. The prices are competitive and the sightseeing is priceless.

Speaking of malls, there are a couple relative newcomers to the Waikiki scene. The largest, **Royal Hawaiian Shopping Center**, spans Kalakaua Avenue all the way from the Royal Hawaiian Hotel to Lewers Street (a stretch so long that some people consider walking it their exercise for the day). Along this four-tiered marathon course you can buy cameras, coral, or ice cream. There are boutiques, banks, sporting good stores, and surf shops; restaurants, jewelry stores, pinball parlors, and practically anything else you could conceive — all in the heart of the heart of Waikiki.

The other newcomer, **Waikiki Trade Center**, is located along Kuhio Avenue between Seaside Avenue and Duke's Lane. A remarkable steel-and-mirror structure adorned with stained-glass windows, it features some equally elegant shops. **Following Sea** (926-1808) is here with an inspiring collection of handcrafted goods, from textiles to ceramics to woodcarvings. This store (and its branches in greater Honolulu and elsewhere) represents over 350 craftspeople from across the United States. The **Waikiki Trade Center** also houses chic clothing and jewelry shops, plus a sidewalk cafe, **The Grape Escape** (923-0438), where you can finish off a hard day shopping with a cappuchino or a glass of wine.

The large hotels usually contain shopping plazas too. Foremost among these are **Hemmeter Center** in the Hyatt Regency Waikiki (2424 Kalakaua Avenue) and the **Rainbow Bazaar** at the Hilton Hawaiian Village (2005 Kalia Road). The Hyatt's complex, a triple-tiered arcade, contains some of Hawaii's smartest shops. Like the Hilton facility, it is *the* place when you're looking for the very best. There are fine art shops, designer apparel stores, gem shops, and more. For glamour and style, these hotel centers are unbeatable.

GREATER HONOLULU

Ala Moana Center, on the outskirts of Waikiki (1450 Ala Moana Boulevard), is reputedly one of the world's largest shopping centers. This multitiered complex has practically everything. Where most self-respecting malls have one department store, Ala Moana has four: **Sears** (947-0211), **Penney's** (946-8068), Hawaii's own **Liberty House** (941-2345), and a Japanese emporium called **Shirokiya** (941-9111). There's also a **Woolworth's** (941-3005) and **Long's Drug Store** (941-4433), both good places to buy inexpensive Hawaiian curios. For imported goods you might try **India Imports International** (949-5777), **Philippine Handicrafts** (949-7611), or **Hotei-Ya** (949-6838). You'll also find an assortment of stores selling liquor, antiques, tennis and golf supplies, stationery, leather goods, cameras, shoes, art, tobacco, etc., etc., etc.

And, in a paragraph by itself, there's **Honolulu Book Shop** (941-2274). Together with its sister store downtown at 190 South King Street, this is Hawaii's finest bookstore. Both branches contain excellent selections of Hawaiian books, bestsellers, paperbacks, magazines, and out-of-town newspapers.

Ala Moana may be the biggest, but **Ward Warehouse** is the most interesting shopping center around. Located on Ala Moana Boulevard between Waikiki and downtown Honolulu, it's worth visiting if only for one store — **Rare Discovery** (524-4811). Filled with ingenious decorations and unique art, this is the most fascinating shop I've ever entered. You've probably seen glass menageries and wood jigsaw puzzles, but how about ceramic penguins or batik triptychs? There are kinetic wall sculptures (such as wooden clocks with gears exposed), stuffed animals, and even stuffed plants.

There are also stylish boutiques in this shopping complex, plus a place called **Exhibit Exhibit Exhibit** (531-2278) that sells locally-made ceramics. And don't bypass the **Artist Guild** (531-2933), selling batiks, pen-and-ink drawings, stained glass, photographs, and other works by island artisans; or **The Art Board** (521-6203), featuring outstanding posters. Then, for that post-buying spree let-down, you can perk up with a cappuchino or espresso at the cleverly tagged **Coffee, Tea, Or...?** (524-3066).

Scattered around town are several other shops that I recommend you check out. **Cost Less Imports**, at 2525 South King Street near the University of Hawaii's Manoa campus, has a warehouse full of bargains from all over the world. It's a great place to pick up wickerware, ceramics, and handcrafted items.

At **Lanakila Crafts** (1809 Bachelot Street; 531-0555) most of the goods are made by some local disabled folks, and the craftsmanship is superb. There are shell necklaces, woven handbags, monkeypod bowls, and homemade dolls. You'll probably see these items in other stores around the islands, with much higher price tags than here at the "factory."

The **Foundry Arts Center** (899 Waimanu; 538-7288) consists of a network of artisans producing ceramics, metal sculptures, jewelry, stained glass, photographs, paintings, and leather goods. It's a very informal affair: you can tour the workshops and sometimes bargain with craftspeople for their wares.

If you're seeking Asian items, then Chinatown is the place. Spotted throughout this tumbledown sector are small shops selling statuettes, pottery, woodcrafts, and other curios. It's also worthwhile wandering through the **Cultural Plaza**, on the corner of Beretania Street and Mauna Kea. This mall is filled with Asian jewelers, bookstores, and knickknack shops.

For secondhand items you might try the flea market at the **Kam Drive-In Theatre** (98-850 Moanalua Road). It's a great place to barter for bargains, meet local folks, and find items you'll never see in stores. Open Wednesday, Thursday, Saturday, and Sunday.

If, on the other hand, you'd prefer shopping in a space-age setting, there's nothing to match **Pearlridge Center**. Situated several miles west of Honolulu, overlooking Pearl Harbor, it's modernistic to an extreme. There are actually two centers here, connected by a monorail which continually streams across the grounds carrying shoppers from Pearlridge's "Phase 1" to "Phase 2." Within these twin centers are several major department stores, two bookstores, and corridor upon corridor, level upon level, of other shops. As the local crowds will attest, it's an outstanding place to shop.

There's another suburban shopping center, **Kahala Mall**, located on the other side of Honolulu. You'll find it a few miles *diamondhead* of the city in the fashionable Kahala district. Featuring a number of designer-name shops, this is where Honolulu's well-heeled residents go for fashions. Nevertheless, the mall is also a choice spot for knickknacks, notions, and such.

With all these shops, stands, malls, and markets to select from, you may find that your Honolulu holiday involves as much shopping as swimming. But if the spirit so wills—why not?

WHAT TO BUY

The best way to keep the memory of a Hawaiian sojourn alive forever is to take a piece of the islands home with you. Of course, there are certain precautions that must be taken (and I'm not just talking about those recommended by the Better Business Bureau). Hawaii, you see, is an exotic and singular place, with mythic traditions that can influence even innocent shoppers. You must remember, for instance, never to take a lava piece home, because removing that sacred rock from her shores will incur the wrath of Madame Pele, goddess of volcanoes. A better way to find that special remembrance is to browse through Honolulu's countless shops and pick out a unique island souvenir.

Jewelry always makes a memorable keepsake, and Hawaii's tropical environment provides unusual materials for creating body ornaments. **Coral**, a delicate organism which divers retrieve offshore, is fashioned into colorful necklaces. **Kukui nuts**, those hard, lustrous objects which ancient Polynesians used to light their torches, are fabricated into *leis* and pendants. There are also shells of every imaginable size and shape, including the **puka shell** with its natural hole, which make fashionable jewelry. A recent innovation involves **maile leaves**, formerly a symbol of Hawaiian royalty, which are dipped in gold and worn as pendants. That gilded metal can also be cast into bracelets or rings with your name inscribed in Hawaiian.

The stunning hardwoods that grow in the island's lush forests are also vital materials for local artisans. **Koa, milo**, and **monkeypod**, among the more outstanding, are fashioned into bowls, figurines, and furniture.

The tropical countryside produces other memories in the form of Polynesian plants and flowers, which can be mailed or taken home on the plane. **Orchids, birds of paradise, anthuriums, hibiscus**, and **ti** plants grow in colorful profusion throughout the islands. Be sure to buy specially inspected plants because you will be required to pass through an agricultural checkpoint before departing Hawaii.

Tropical foods, delicious as they are, will simply not be around long enough to become keepsakes, but nevertheless they make memorable presents. Local distributors can have boxes of pineapples and papayas waiting for you at the airport; or you might want to say *aloha* to a friend back home with a message inscribed on coconut, better known as a **coconote**. Then there are island **jams** and **jellies**— guava, papaya, mango—sold singly and in packaged assortments. Or how about **macadamia nuts**, those delicious morsels grown on the Big Island and prepared as salted snacks or chocolate-covered confections? Another specialty item that comes courtesy of the Big Island is **Kona coffee**, an especially aromatic brew that happens to be the only coffee commercially grown in the United States. For those with adventurous palates there's **cracked seed**, a preserved fruit introduced to Hawaii by the Chinese. Ranging from sweet to sour, cracked seed flavors include cherry, mango, plum, apricot, lemon, and lime. The seed of each fruit is crushed and then pickled to release and preserve the flavor.

Everyone is familiar with Hawaiian fashions, and it's a rare visitor who departs the islands without adding a **muumuu** or **aloha shirt** to the wardrobe. Evocative of the tropics, these local garments feature striking designs and brilliant colors. One highly unusual cloth, **tapa**, is made from mulberry bark. Imported from Tonga and Samoa, it is used for purses, hats, and wallhangings. You'll also find hats and slippers woven from **lauhala**, the leaf of the pandanus tree.

The spirit of Hawaii, it seems, is alive and thriving in the marketplace. The islands' many artisans and importers are capable of satisfying even the most discerning shopper. In addition to handicrafts, plants, and food, you can purchase **records** produced by local performers and **books** filled with the lore and history of Hawaii. Together they'll evoke memories of those pearly sands and *aloha* days long after you've left Honolulu's city lights behind. So if you're searching out that special gift, or just after a personal remembrance, Hawaii will provide a basketful of shopping ideas.

Nightlife

Honolulu is the nightlife capital of the Pacific. Not only is it the biggest city for thousands of miles, but a Polynesian oasis and cultural crossroads as well. The entertainment, not surprisingly, is a medley of sights, sounds, and spectacular events. Outside Las Vegas, or perhaps Los Angeles, night owls would be hard pressed to find a more scintillating scene.

Headlining Waikiki's waterfront clubs are mainland stars, pop musicians, pidgin-speaking comedians, Hawaiian soloists, and Polynesian dancers. Musically there's everything from traditional Hawaiian slack key guitar to New Wave and disco. You'll encounter hula shows, cabarets, Polynesian revues, rock singers, and ukelele plunkers. There are beachfront watering holes where you can relax and watch the moon over Diamond Head, or swinging clubs ablaze with lights and activity until four in the morning. All packed, tight as gunpowder, into this city by the sea.

For an explosive night, or a silent, candlelit evening, consider the descriptions below. They provide a thumbnail sketch of the events and entertainers that comprise Honolulu's long list of happenings.

CLUBS AND CABARETS

For a quiet drink in a cozy atmosphere, I recommend **The Library** (2552 Kalakaua; 922-6611). This relaxing piano bar is located in the Hawaiian Regent Hotel, next door to the renowned Third Floor Restaurant. It's a choice spot to sit back and recollect at the end of an enervating day. Good drinks, good service—who could ask for more?

Trappers, nestled in a corner of the plush Hyatt Regency Hotel (2424 Kalakaua Avenue; 922-9292), is another intimate bar. It's a split-level affair, beautifully appointed, with private booths. The music is low-key, the mood mellow, and the staff congenial.

One place that almost always headlines talented Hawaiian bands is the **Kaamaina Room** at the Ala Moana Hotel (410 Atkinson Drive; 955-4811). This nightclub caters to local residents rather than tourists, so the music, like the crowd, is homegrown. No cover; two-drink minimum.

At the other end of the spectrum, over by the University of Hawaii's Manoa campus, there's **Wilde Oscar's** (in Puck's

Alley, corner of University Avenue and South King Street; 947-1857). The rock music is live and lively every night from 7 till 2. There's a large dance floor with a mirror that doubles the distance, plus an L-shaped bar where you'll sometimes find people wading three deep. Since it's located in the very heart of the campus community, Wilde Oscar's draws a young, vivacious crowd. Even on weeknights (when a cover charge prevails), you're liable to find the roof barely remaining in place.

To hit the hottest club in Honolulu, head back toward Waikiki to **Da Sting** (in the Princess Kaiulani Hotel, 120 Kaiulani Avenue; 923-5556). With several bars, a spacious dance floor, and *da kine* crowds, this disco is *da* place. There's live music nightly, usually a local band copying several Top-40 disco groups. The last time I made it by, the place was heel-to-toe with dancers, and crowds were queuing up outside.

Waikiki is definitely disco central. Every big hotel seems to have converted a dusty ballroom or sluggish restaurant into a throbbing strobe-lit dance hall. **Spat's**, the Hyatt Regency's (2424 Kalakaua Avenue; 922-9292) contribution to the latest dance craze, is the poshest. With stuffed chairs, oil paintings, and stained glass, it looks more the part of a fashionable restaurant. And until the deejay cranks up his victrola nightly at 10, that's exactly what it is. But after the witching hour, anything goes. No cover, no minimum; dress slacks and closed-toe shoes required.

The Point After (Hawaiian Regent Hotel, 2552 Kalakaua Avenue; 922-6611) is another hot young club. A band and deejay alternate sets. As you might guess from the name, the design motif is football, with more flashing lights than an exploding scoreboard. There is a cover charge.

After The Point After you can count on **Infinity** (Sheraton Hotel, 2255 Kalakaua Avenue; 922-5566) for an equally ecstatic light show and a similar mix of band and deejay sounds. Cover charge and two-drink minimum.

Also for your dancing pleasure, though on a quieter note, is the **Hanohano Room** of the Sheraton Waikiki (2255 Kalakaua Avenue; 922-4422). Overlooking Waikiki from high atop this splendid hotel, it's the perfect place for soft moods and slow dances.

There's tea dancing every Saturday in the Royal Hawaiian Hotel's luxurious **Monarch Room** (2259 Kalakaua Avenue;

(923-7311). Since the Royal Hawaiian was Honolulu's poshest hotel back in the thirties, it's well-suited for a nostalgic return to the Big Band era.

You can also soft shoe across the dance floor at the **Maile Lounge** of the Kahala Hilton Hotel (5000 Kahala Avenue; 734-2211).

The gay scene centers at several clubs around Waikiki's Kuhio Avenue. **Hamburger Mary's** (2109 Kuhio Avenue; 922-6722) is the most dynamic. There's no dancing, just drinking and carousing. It's simply a U-shaped bar with a side patio, but the place draws huge crowds.

Together with **Hula's Bar and Lei Stand** (923-0669) next door, it forms an unbeatable duo. Hula's, a disco complete with strobe-lit dance floor, rocks until 2 a.m. Cover charge.

The Honolulu red-light scene centers around Hotel Street in Chinatown. This sleazy, run-down strip is lined with hostess bars and adult book stores. Prostitutes, straight and gay, are on the street regularly.

Well-heeled prostitutes work Waikiki around Kalakaua Avenue and near the big hotels. The trade here is much more tourist-oriented. Along Hotel Steet it's aimed primarily at sailors.

DINNER SHOWS

Combining dinner with an evening of entertainment is a favored format among many Honolulu club owners. The tab runs higher, but the arrangement takes care of your entire night, from soup to encore. If you'd prefer to independently choose a restaurant, but still want to see the entertainer featured in a "dinner show," you might make reservations for the later "cocktail show." You'll hear the same program, but pay only for a cover charge and drink minimum.

Most of Honolulu's top performers appear in dinner shows. Three in particular, whose names are synonymous with island entertainment, will require you to settle in for supper or drop by later at cocktail time.

Don Ho, Hawaii's own Mr. "Tiny Bubbles," headlines a nightly bill at the **International Market Place** (2330 Kalakaua Avenue; 923-0211). Don, who cavorts with the audience onstage and mixes a few barbs in with his Hawaiian melodies, is a local institution. Crooning all the favorites from "Blue Hawaii" to "Beyond the Reef," he's particularly popular with older folks.

The **Hilton Hawaiian Village** (2005 Kalia Road; 949-4321) spotlights Jim Nabors. You might remember him in his television role as Gomer Pyle. He's hilarious as ever, but nowadays Jim adds a classical baritone voice to those comedy routines. To top it off, his show features a spectacular cast of singers and dancers.

The drawing card at the **Kahala Hilton** (5000 Kahala Avenue; 734-2211) is a *kaamaaina* named Danny Kaleikini. Kaleikini has been the hotel centerpiece for well over a decade now and still attracts crowds with his Hawaiian songs and charming humor. He's a triple threat on stage—singing, dancing and playing enough instruments to fill an island orchestra. Danny can work out on the drums, ukulele, even the nose flute.

The **Monarch Room** of the Royal Hawaiian Hotel (2259 Kalakaua Avenue; 923-7311) parades a variety of top entertainers across the stage of its popular evening shows.

LUAUS

Naturally the most Hawaiian of dinner shows are those involving a *luau*. These Polynesian feasts are a traditional aspect of island life. During Hawaii's royal era, islanders filled an underground oven, or *imu*, with steaming lava rocks and baked a ceremonial pig. Then they added fish, *poi*, and breadfruit dishes, mixed a narcotic potion labeled *awa*, and threw a party.

Today several Honolulu caterers, with variations on the ancient theme, sponsor *luaus* regularly. Old Polynesian practices are combined with modern Hawaiian pleasures (like drinking mai tais and pina coladas), and entertainment—in the form of troupes of firewalkers, hula dancers, and island altos—is added. The result is an all-you-can-eat, all-you-can-drink extravaganza.

For a more traditional Hawaiian feast, consult the newspaper listings for church and other local groups that regularly sponsor *luaus*. But if you're willing to go whole hog on a slam bang tourist event, one of the programs below should prove the perfect ticket.

Germaine's Luau (949-6626), reputedly the best, happens every evening on a beach outside Honolulu. A torchlight ceremony and exhibition of the art of fishnet throwing are followed by a multicourse dinner and Polynesian show.

Chuck Machado's Luau (836-0249), featuring a native feast and a troupe of Polynesian performers, is presented regularly at the beachfront Outrigger Hotel or in Honolulu's Paradise Park.

Every Sunday the **Royal Hawaiian Hotel** (923-7311) sponsors a torchlit Waikiki Beach *luau*; while the **Kahala Hilton** (734-2211) hosts a *hukilau* that combines a ceremonial fishnetting party with a *luau*.

POLYNESIAN REVUES

Close cousin to the *luau* is the Polynesian revue. These gala affairs generally combine a buffet dinner with an evening's entertainment. Drawing on cuisines and cultures from all across the Pacific, the event begins with an assortment of exotic drinks and dishes. The show following will often feature firewalkers and dancers from such far-flung archipelagoes as Fiji and Tonga. Musically it will visit Samoa, Tahiti, Maori New Zealand, etc.; by curtain call you'll have experienced the more exotic aspects of Polynesian life.

Many of the major revues are centered in the large hotels along Waikiki Beach. Among the foremost is **Tavana's Polynesian Spectacular** (923-2955) at the Moana Hotel. Tavana has drawn his cast, over three dozen costumed entertainers, from Tahiti, Samoa, the Marquesas, and Fiji. In a beautiful banyan-protected courtyard overlooking the beach, they present island songs while performing hulas and knife dances.

Tihati's South Seas Spectacular (922-4646), staged nearby at the Waikiki Beachcomber Hotel, features a Samoan fire dance as well as other dances and songs from across the Pacific.

There's also **Kalo's South Seas Revue** (941-5205), on the grounds of the Ala Moana Hotel just outside Waikiki. Kalo herself performs a fire dance while the troupe presents a medley of Polynesian tunes.

You might recognize **Al Harrington—The South Pacific Man** (House of Lono; 524-6771) more readily as Ben Kokua from television's "Hawaii Five-O." Today the erstwhile detective unravels cultures and customs in a talking tour of Polynesia. Al, who despite the Irish moniker is full-blooded Samoan, appears with an ensemble of talented entertainers.

The Polynesian Cultural Center, located on Oahu's Windward Coast, extends an **Invitation to Paradise** (293-8561) almost every night. Featuring a cast of dozens, from all over the Pacific, the show includes a waterborne revue and a musical trip through the history of Polynesia.

ENTERTAINERS

There are two ways to determine an evening's entertainment. The first, detailed above, is to choose a nightclub; the second is to select a particular entertainer. Whichever technique you follow, Honolulu will accommodate with a welter of choices.

Best way to decide upon an entertainer is to check the newspaper listings. The islands are chockablock with talented performers; at any particular time, many will be appearing at nightspots around town.

Browsing the local papers, you'll find that Hawaii's ancient musical tradition is alive and well, nurtured by a number of individuals who perform their own compositions as well as old Polynesian songs. Topping this Hawaiian hit parade are the **Brothers Cazimero**, a local duo that performs some of the most enchanting island songs you're likely ever to experience. Roland and Robert Cazimero write most of their own material, heavily influenced by Polynesian melodies, and have already produced several albums.

Several soloists—including **Loyal Garner, Melveen Leed**, and **Genoa Keawe**—will also carry you back to Hawaii of yore. On the ukelele, no one matches **Herb Ohta**. **The Sons of Niihau**, an all-Hawaiian ensemble, also follow this old school.

If you're interested in catching these classic sounds, but want to hear the musicians before paying to see them, tune in KCCN at 1420 on the radio dial. It's an outstanding all-Hawaiian station that serves as the home of island soul.

Honolulu also features vibrantly modern Hawaiian music. There are numerous entertainers and ensembles that mix the plunky ukulele sounds familiar to tourists with strains of jazz and rock to create a hybrid Hawaiian sound. The island's top name entertainers are part of this "Blue Hawaii"—"Beyond the Reef" tradition. Several—**Don Ho, Jim Nabors**, and **Danny Kaleikini**—are described in the "Dinner Shows" section above. **The Aliis**, a six-man group that often backs up Don Ho, fits this mold, as does a band named **Society of Seven**.

Several other groups, more heavily influenced by pop music, form the young vanguard of this modern Hawaiian sound. Included among these electric ensembles are **Keola and Kapono Beamer, Olomana, Kalapana**, and the **Peter Moon Band**.

Also be sure to catch a show by one of the island's brilliant comedians. **Andy Bumatai, Rap Reiplinger**, and **Frank DeLima**, who mix pidgin slang into their rapid-fire monologues, manage to hilariously mock all Hawaii's ethnic groups (as well as island visitors) without insulting anyone. Andy is the most popular among these standup comics, but each presents a marvelous show that will draw you in to the humorous aspects of island life.

SUNSET CRUISES

These events, which provide an evening's entertainment while exploring the Honolulu coastline, are described in the "Sightseeing" section below.

Addresses and Phone Numbers

HONOLULU AND WAIKIKI

Ambulance—(911)
Barber Shop—Waikiki Barber Shop, 2863 Kalakaua Avenue (923-0374)
Better Business Bureau—677 Ala Moana Boulevard #614 (531-8131)
Books—Honolulu Book Shops, Ala Moana Center or 190 South King Street (941-2274 or 537-6224)
Bus Schedule—(531-1611)
Churches—Hawaii Council of Churches, 200 North Vineyard Boulevard (521-2666)
City Information Office — (523-4385)
Coast Guard (search and rescue emergencies) — (536-4336)
Dentist Information Bureau — (536-2135)
Federal Information Center — (546-8620)
Fire Department — (911)
Fishing Supplies — K. Kaya Fishing Supplies, 901 Kekaulike (538-1578)
Hardware — Oahu Lumber and Hardware Co., 1217 North King Street (845-3961)
Hawaii Visitors Bureau — 2270 Kalakaua Avenue (923-1811)
Hospital — Queen's Hospital, 1301 Punchbowl (538-9011)
Laundromat — Outrigger Laundromat, 2335 Kalakaua Avenue (923-0711)
Library — 478 South King Street (548-4775)
Liquor — Liquors-Gourmet Bazaar, International Market Place, 2330 Kalakaua Avenue (923-7658)
Parks — Department of Parks and Recreation (523-4525); Division of State Parks (548-7455)
Pharmacy — Long's Drugs, Ala Moana Center, 1450 Ala Moana Boulevard (941-4433)
Photo Supply — Francis Camera Shop, Ala Moana Center, 1450 Ala Moana Boulevard (946-2879)
Police Department — 1455 South Beretania Street (911)
Post Office — 330 Saratoga Road (941-1062)
State Information Office — (548-6222)
Suicide and Crisis Center — (521-4555)
Surf Report — (836-1952)
Taxi — Charley's Taxi (531-1333); Sida Taxi (836-0011)
Visitor Information Program — (836-6413)
Weather Report — (836-0234)

CHAPTER IV

Honolulu: The Great Outdoors

Sightseeing

Sightseeing in Honolulu is little short of spectacular. Steeped in history, this capital city offers countless relics and monuments as well as places of remarkable natural beauty. If you want to thoroughly tour the city, plan to take several days. Or, if time is limited, you might glance through this section to find just a few places that look particularly interesting. I especially recommend Diamond Head, Mission Houses Museum, Iolani Palace, Chinatown, and the Bishop Museum.

SELF-GUIDED TOURS

DIAMOND HEAD AND WAIKIKI

There could be no more appropriate point to begin a Honolulu tour than the place which has become symbolic of all Hawaii. **Diamond Head,** a 760-foot-tall crater, is the state's most famous landmark. The Hawaiians called it *Leahi,* seeing in its sloping face the brow of an *ahi,* or yellowfin tuna. Nineteenth-century sailors, mistaking its volcanic glass for priceless gems, gave the promontory its present name. If you follow Diamond Head Road around the crater to its inland side, then through the tunnel, you can drive into the crater itself. A foot-path three-quarters of a mile long leads to the crater rim for marvelous views of Honolulu.

Diamond Head marks the east end of **Waikiki.** To sightsee this quarter of Honolulu, head west to **Kapiolani Park**. This 140-acre spread contains a **Rose Garden** as well as jogging tracks, tennis courts, picnic areas, and so on. It also includes the **Waikiki Aquarium** (nominal admission) with a fascinating tropical fish collection, and the **Honolulu Zoo**, which houses many tropical birds.

Another feature of Kapiolani Park is the Waikiki Shell, a Polynesian-style amphitheater, where any Tuesday through Friday at 10 a.m. you can see the free **Kodak Hula Show**. Featuring singers, dancers, and musicians, the show is a favorite among visitors. If you've ever yearned to learn the hula, this is the place.

Along busy Kalakaua Avenue, a favorite nesting place for construction cranes, are two old hotels. The **Moana Hotel**, built in 1901, was one of Waikiki's earliest high-rises. Its wood-frame structure, vaulted ceilings, and large rooms represent the days when Hawaii was strictly a rich man's retreat. The nearby **Royal Hawaiian Hotel** is Hawaii's "pink palace," a Spanish baroque-style caravansary constructed in 1927. With its intricate gardens, arcades, and balconies, this is Waikiki's most interesting edifice.

Of course, a tour of Waikiki is not complete without a stroll through the **shopping malls** (see the "Shopping" section in the preceding chapter) and a walk along the **beach** (see the "Beaches and Parks" section).

DOWNTOWN HONOLULU

From this busy enclave it's a short drive, but a long walk, to the center of Honolulu. On the way downtown there are several points of interest. **Kewalo Basin** (or **Fisherman's Wharf**) on Ala Moana Boulevard is home port for sampans and sport fishing boats. The **Honolulu Academy of Arts** (900 South Beretania Street) often displays the James Michener collection of woodblocks from Japan, plus works by old masters and young locals. And if you'd like to see a Sunday church service delivered in Hawaiian, attend **Ke Alaula O Ka Malamalama Church** (910 Cooke Street).

Your tour of historic downtown Honolulu can begin with the oldest wooden house in the islands. **Mission Houses** Museum (553 South King Street; admission charged), dating to the first missionaries, contains a **Frame House** prefabricated in New England and erected here in 1821. This Yankee-style structure sheltered newly arrived missionary families. The nearby **Chamberlain Depository** was constructed of local coral in 1831 and used primarily as a storehouse. Another coral building, the **Printing House**, rose in 1841 and today contains a replica of the first press to print the Hawaiian language. The **Mission Cemetery**, across the road from these houses, dates to 1823. Together this complex represents a seminal center for the missionaries who made Hawaiian a written language and then rewrote the entire history of Hawaii.

Towering above the cemetery is Honolulu's oldest church, **Kawaiahao Church**. Built of coral and timber in 1842, this imposing cathedral became Hawaii's mother church, where kings were christened, inaugurated, and mourned. Services are still performed here in Hawaiian and English every Sunday at 10:30 a.m.

Across South King Street, that brick structure with the stately white pillars is the **Mission Memorial Building**, constructed in 1916 to honor the early church leaders. The nearby Renaissance-style building with the tile roof is **Honolulu Hale**, the City Hall. You might want to venture into the central courtyard, an open-air plaza surrounded by stone columns.

Continue down South King Street toward the center of Honolulu. **Iolani Palace** will be on your right. Built for King Kalakaua in 1882, this beautiful Renaissance-style mansion served as the royal residence until Queen Liliuokalani was overthrown in 1893. Following the abortive 1895 restoration, the ill-starred monarch was imprisoned here. It later became the capitol building for the Territory of Hawaii, and today is the only royal palace in the United States. Also on the palace grounds are the **Iolani Barracks**, built in 1871 to station the Royal Household Guards, and the **Bandstand**, constructed for King Kalakaua's 1883 coronation. You can wander the royal grounds free; there's an admission fee to tour the palace, which is open Wednesday through Saturday. Children under five are not admitted.

Behind the palace rises the **State Capitol Building** in all its modern magnificence. Surrounded by flared pillars which resemble palm trees, this exquisite structure represents a variety of Hawaiian themes. A statue of Father Damien, the leper martyr of Molokai, stands at the entrance. The House and Senate chambers are cone-shaped to resemble volcanoes. The open-air courtyard reflects the state's balmy weather.

Back on South King Street, across from Iolani Palace, stands the **King Kamehameha Statue**, a huge gilt-and-bronze figure cast in Italy. Unveiled for Kalakaua's inauguration, this statue is actually a replica of the original, which rests in Kapaau on the Big Island. Behind Kamehameha is **Aliiolani Hale**, the **Judiciary Building**, which was completed in 1874 and originally housed the Hawaiian Parliament.

For a tour of Honolulu's waterfront, go left on Richards Street toward Pier Five where the **Falls of Clyde** is berthed. This century-old sailing ship plied the Pacific carrying sugar and oil. Built in Scotland, it is reputedly the only fully-rigged four-masted ship in the world. For a small admission you can tour this marvelous floating museum.

From here, follow the roadway along the water to **Aloha Tower**. Anytime from 8 a.m. until 9 p.m. you can elevator up to the tenth-floor observation deck for a crow's-nest view of Honolulu harbor and city.

Back to ground zero, head *mauka* across the highway and up **Fort Street Mall** to Merchant Street. The late-nineteenth and early-twentieth-century buildings along Merchant Steet mark the **old downtown** section of Honolulu's business district.

At the end of Merchant Street take a right on Nuuanu, then a left on Hotel Street for a tour of **Chinatown**. From Hotel Street you can explore side streets and check out the Chinese groceries, medicinal herb shops, import stores, and noodle factories.

This weatherbeaten ghetto, a vital part of Honolulu's history, has long been a center of controversy. When bubonic plague savaged the Chinese community in 1900, the white-led government tried to contain the pestilence by burning down afflicted homes. The bumbling bureaucrats managed to raze most of Chinatown, destroying businesses as well as houses. They later apologized, claiming their intentions had been good. But for years afterward, the Chinese claimed it was all a conspiracy to undermine their position in Honolulu society.

Continuing along Hotel Street across Nuuanu Stream, go right on College Walk and follow it upstream. You'll pass the tile-roofed **Tokyo Theatre**, dating to 1938, and **Izumo Taishakyo Mission**, a Shinto shrine. Up on Vineyard Boulevard you can walk through **Foster Botanic Garden**, a fascinating twenty-acre plot planted with palms, orchids, coffee trees, poisonous plants, and countless exotic species. Then, returning down the other side of Nuuanu Stream, stop and tour the **Cultural Plaza** with its many Oriental shops and displays.

NUUANU AVENUE

If you have a car, or want to do some urban hiking, go from downtown Honolulu up Nuuanu Avenue. Along this busy thoroughfare and its quieter side streets are some strikingly beautiful temples. First is the **Soto Mission of Hawaii** (1708 Nuuanu), home of a meditative Zen sect. Then set in from the road beside a small stream, sits **Honolulu Myohoji Temple** (2003 Nuuanu), capped with a peace tower. Uphill from this Buddhist shrine lies **Honolulu Memorial Park**, a Japanese cemetery (22 Craigside Place). Here you'll find **Kyoto-Kinkakaku-ji**, an ancestral monument bounded on three sides by a carp pond, and the enchanting **Sanju Pagoda**.

Nearby **Tenrikyo Mission** (2236 Nuuanu) is a woodframe temple which was moved here from Japan. Sections of this delicate structure were built without nails. The **Royal Mausoleum**, across the street, is the resting place for many members of the Kamehameha and Kalakaua families, who ruled nineteenth-century Hawaii.

The climax of this side tour is a visit to the most stately temple of all—the home of the **Chinese Buddhist Association of Hawaii** (42 Kawananakoa Place). This grand, multihued edifice contains an elaborate worship place displaying statues of Buddha and other luminaries.

PUNCHBOWL AND TANTALUS

It's only a few miles from downtown Honolulu to **Punchbowl**, the circular crater of a dead volcano. Together with Diamond Head, this is Honolulu's best example of the volcanic action which created Hawaii. Today Punchbowl is the site of the **National Memorial Cemetery**, with the graves of over 20,000 war dead spread across the bottom of the bowl. You can pass through this memorial park up along the crater rim for some breathtaking views of Honolulu.

Then you can explore yet higher by taking Tantalus Drive as it climbs up the side of 2,013-foot **Tantalus**. After winding through a rain forest, this country road becomes Round Top Drive and leads to **Puu Ualakaa Park**, a hilltop retreat with even more exotic Honolulu vistas. Round Top then drops back into the city, completing a scenic loop into Honolulu's hill country.

UNIVERSITY OF HAWAII, MANOA CAMPUS

Located in Manoa Valley about a mile from Waikiki, this is an important cultural and counter-cultural center. With over 20,000 students and 2,000 faculty members, it's an excellent place to meet people. You should certainly visit the **East-West Center**, where there's always an opportunity to encounter foreign students. The center, designed by world-renowned architect I. M. Pei, is devoted to the study of Asian and American cultures.

There's an excellent Hawaiian and Pacific collection in the **Hamilton Library**. Or, if you'd like to stroll the campus, pick up a walking guide to some of the 560 trees and plants growing here (available from the Office of University Relations in Hawaii Hall).

PEARL HARBOR

The United States Navy sponsors free boat tours out to the **U.S.S. Arizona** floating memorial every Tuesday through Saturday from 9 a.m. to 3 p.m. This is an excellent opportunity to view Pearl Harbor, a once-beautiful anchorage which today is surrounded by military installations. The boat ride out to the sunken hulk of the battleship Arizona will take you through an area heavily bombed by the Japanese in the December 7, 1941, sneak attack. The United States lost eighteen ships and over 3,000 men in what became the nation's greatest military disaster. Over 1,100 men were entombed alive in the Arizona. The memorial to those men represents a point of pilgrimage for many visitors to Hawaii, making it the islands' single most popular attraction. Several buses from Ala Moana Center stop regularly at the shuttle boat dock. Before boarding, remember that no bathing suits, barefeet, or children under six are permitted.

THE CROSS-ISLAND EXPRESS

There are several other sightseeing spots on the outskirts of Honolulu. You might want to tour them while traveling along either of the two highways that lead from the city across the Koolau Range to the island's Windward Coast.

Likelike Highway (Route 63) follows this route. Before venturing across the mountains, you'll pass the **Bishop Museum** near the intersection of Routes H-1 and 63. Built around the turn of the century, the museum contains an excellent collection of Hawaiian and Pacific artifacts. There are cultural and historical displays aplenty, plus a planetarium right next door. Quite simply, you must visit the Bishop, one of the finest museums of its kind in the world. There are royal feather capes, outrigger canoes, primitive artworks, thrones, crowns, and similarly fascinating natural history exhibits. To complement this education in things Polynesian, the museums's **Atherton Halau** (847-3511, ext. 106) offers classes in quilting, weaving, *lei*-making, and hula. Admission fees are charged for the museum and classes.

The other, more scenic, cross-mountain route is the Pali Highway (Route 61), which passes several points of interest. The first is **Queen Emma's Summer Palace**. Built in 1843 and used as a retreat by King Kamehameha IV and his wife, this white-pillared house is now a museum. For a small admission fee, you can view the Queen's personal artifacts as well as other period pieces. Tree-shaded **Nuuanu Valley Park** adjoins the estate. Then, for a tour through this exotically forested valley, turn onto **Nuuanu Pali Drive** and follow it until it rejoins the highway.

Farther up, there's a turnoff to **Nuuanu Pali Lookout**, a vista point that should not be missed! Without doubt, this is Oahu's finest view. You can scan the rugged face of the Koolau cliffs as they knife-edge 3,000 feet down to a gently rolling coastal shelf. The view extends from Makapuu Point to the last reaches of Kaneohe Bay, and from the cliff rim far out to sea. It was over this precipice that Kamehameha I drove his enemies when he conquered Oahu in 1795.

GUIDED TOURS

It sometimes seems that Honolulu has more tour operators than tourists. From points all around Waikiki, buses, vans, limousines, and cabs set out every day in every direction. Searching for well-known points, they visit some of Oahu's most fascinating and beautiful spots. In the process, they help introduce visitors to Hawaii while providing a general overview of Honolulu and the rest of Oahu.

But there are many outstanding sights these tours overlook, and others that they touch upon much too briefly. Personally, my favorite method of sightseeing is with a group of friends in a rental car. When I do sign up for a guided tour, I book myself on a small van rather than one of the large tourist buses. Then I make future arrangements to visit independently the places I particularly liked on the guided tour. So the official tour serves as a way to get my bearings and determine where I'd like to spend the rest of my vacation.

Of course, some people don't drive; others simply enjoy the camaraderie and carefree nature of guided tours, and feel that the bigger the group the better. Whatever your disposition toward tours, you'll certainly find at least one in Honolulu that fits your purse, personality, and plans.

STANDARD TOURS

Both the large bus companies and the small minibus operators offer narrated tours of Honolulu and Oahu. The **circle island tour**, which takes all day, will carry you past the Pali Lookout, Diamond Head, Hanauma Bay, the Windward Coast, Sunset Beach, Pearl Harbor, and numerous other points. There are several variations on the half-day **city tour**, each of which touches down at a few of the following Honolulu locales: Iolani Palace, State Capitol Building, Chinatown, U.S.S. Arizona Memorial, and Punchbowl Crater.

The major bus companies conducting such tours include **Gray Line Hawaii** (922-0400), **Robert's Hawaii Tours** (947-3939), **Charley's Scenic Tours** (955-3381), **Hawaiian Discovery Tours** (945-6495), and **Tradewind Tours** (923-2071).

Van tours for small groups are sponsored by **E Noa Tours** (941-6608), **Polynesian Adventure Tours** (922-0888), **Kiwi Tours** (922-2228), and **Akamai Tours** (922-6485). In addition to the sightseeing circuits described above, these outfits run nature tours for those interested in swimming and snorkeling, riding a glass-bottom boat, or viewing the gardens of Oahu.

SPECIAL TOURS

A number of local companies and civic organizations lead limited tours to places of particular interest in and around Honolulu. Perhaps the most widely recognized is the **Diplo-**

mat's Passport to Polynesia (847-3511). Conducted by the prestigious Bishop Museum, this narrated tour carries you aboard a double-decker London bus to the museum, its planetarium and theater, then to the Mission Houses Museum in downtown Honolulu.

A Walking Tour of Historic Honolulu (531-0481) begins every weekday morning at that same Mission Houses Museum and wends through old Honolulu's most fascinating buildings. Either tour will carry you back to the halcyon days of royal Hawaii.

Chinatown Walking Tours are led by several organizations, including the Chinese Chamber of Commerce (533-3181). After strolling past noodle shops, herb stores, temples, open-air markets, and other spots around this exotic neighborhood, you can relax over a Cantonese-style lunch.

On the University of Hawaii's free **East-West Center Tour** (948-7623) you'll encounter folks from across Asia and the Pacific. The Center is an important multicultural research facility; for the visitor it offers a Japanese garden, teahouse, beautifully landscaped grounds, and a Korean Studies building modeled after a fourteenth-century palace.

The **Foster Garden Tour** (538-7258) meanders through one of Honolulu's loveliest flower collections and provides an insight into the uses and historical importance of many Polynesian plants. No admission fee charged.

And for a lesson in home industry, sign up for the **Dole Cannery Tour** (536-3411), where you'll watch the process and enjoy the product at the world's largest pineapple cannery. Or visit nearby **Hilo Hattie's Fashion Center** (537-2926) for a free look at island designs in the making.

SKY TOURS

Hawaii from the air is the most dramatic scene imaginable. If your flight from the mainland arrives during daylight hours, a fleet of islands, anchored two thousand miles from the nearest shore, will sail into view below you. Guarded by mountain crags and sheer cliffs, they first appear to be floating fortresses. Then, as the plane sweeps inland, those adze-like peaks are softened by lacy waterfalls and flowering gorges.

From a jet all this occurs in a supersonic flash, so several small airline and helicopter companies provide longer, more leisurely, flightseeing tours of the islands. **Air Hawaii** (833-

1122), **Hawaiian Air Tour Service** (923-6577), and **Panorama Air Tour** (836-2122), flying propeller planes, tour all the islands in a single day, usually landing at several of the larger ones. They also offer charter service.

Scenic these flights certainly are, but the best way to see the islands is by helicopter. Outfits like **Kenai Air Hawaii** (836-2071) and **Paradise Helicopters** (955-7861) feature a whirlybird's eye view of Hawaii. Usually they'll just visit one island; if you depart from Honolulu they'll explore Oahu, dusting the mountain tops and soaring right into canyons. Be forewarned: it will be an expensive experience, but one that will float back in your memories long after that gentle bird lands.

Up on Oahu's North Shore, at Dillingham Airfield, you can soar along the mountains and coastline on a **Glider Ride** (623-6711).

CRUISES

With the sea all around, it seems a sin to visit Hawaii without sailing at least once. The suggested way to do so, of course, is aboard your private yacht, or perhaps on a dear friend's oceangoing sloop. If you've left your schooner at home, the next best thing is to sign up for passage aboard one of the many catamarans that cruise the Honolulu waterfront. They may be slightly crowded and noisy, but they'll never lack for conviviality.

SUNSET CRUISES

Several companies sponsor evening sails. With the sun setting dramatically over the ocean, they cruise along Waikiki to Diamond Head. In addition to the incredible vistas, during the two- or three-hour voyage you'll be granted every creature comfort possible—dinner, an open bar, and live entertainment.

Aikane Catamarans (538-3680) and **Hula Kai Catamaran** (524-1800) host these twin-hulled adventures; **Windjammer Cruises** (521-0036) features dinner outings aboard a modern four-masted ship.

PEARL HARBOR CRUISES

Several boats, fully equipped with restaurant and bar, provide tours along Honolulu's spectacular shoreline to Pearl Harbor. During the voyage a narrator will point out interesting sights at this strategic naval base while recounting the story of December 7, 1941. Unfortunately, you won't be able to go inside the U.S.S. Arizona Memorial; only the official Navy tours (described earlier) include a visit to this fascinating museum. Since the Navy tour is not only more inclusive, but free as well, I don't recommend the commercial cruises; if you are interested nevertheless, contact **First Pearl Harbor Cruise** (536-3641) or **Hawaiian Cruises** (923-2061).

GLASS-BOTTOM BOAT CRUISES

For a view of the colorful reefs and tropical fish just off Honolulu's coast, you can sail aboard **Hawaiian Cruises**' (537-1958) glass-bottom boat. This ingenious craft will also provide you an oceanside peek at Honolulu's skyline.

The Sporting Life

With luxurious parks, mountain retreats, and deserted beaches, the area surrounding Honolulu is a paradise for sports lovers. Because of Oahu's varied terrain and microenvironments, it's possible to experience all kinds of outdoor adventures. Within easy driving distance of Honolulu, for instance, you can hike through a steaming rain forest filled with tropical flowers, then descend to a curving white-sand beach populated only by shorebirds and tropical fish.

Paradise, of course, means more than physical beauty. It also involves something called easy living. After you've arrived in Honolulu and begun slowing down from the frantic pace of mainland life, you'll discover that island existence is very relaxing. The style of living is easy and comfortable, yet exciting. You can do absolutely nothing (and find yourself remarkably content), or take off in pursuit of Hawaii's many outdoor adventures.

For those seeking the latter, Oahu features numerous sporting activities for participants and spectators alike. You can hike, camp, swim, play golf and tennis, pick wild fruit, and even scuba dive; or you can sit back to watch local folks gathering shellfish and championship surfers challenging twenty-foot waves. Many Honolulu-area sports are described below. If you're feeling energetic you might want to try some; if not, you can gain an insight into what Hawaiians have been doing for centuries, and may still be doing today just beyond your hotel window.

WATER SPORTS

For swimming, surfing, and skin diving, there's no place quite like Hawaii. With endless miles of white-sand beach, the islands attract aquatic enthusiasts from all over the world. They come to enjoy Hawaii's colorful coral reefs and matchless surf conditions. The how and where of Honolulu watersports are described below. Before taking the plunge, however, there are a few things you should know.

Many water lovers never realize how awesome the sea can be. Particularly on Oahu, where waves regularly reach twenty-foot heights, the ocean is sometimes as treacherous as it is spectacular. Over thirty people a year drown in Hawaii, many others are dragged from the crushing surf with broken backs, and countless numbers sustain cuts and bruises.

These accidents can be entirely avoided if you relate to the ocean with a respect for its power as well as an appreciation of its beauty. All you have to do is heed a few simple guidelines. First, never turn your back on the sea. Waves come in sets: one group may be small and quite harmless, but the next set could be large enough to sweep you out to sea. Never swim alone, and don't swim for at least an hour after eating.

Don't try to surf, or even bodysurf, until you're familiar with the sports' techniques and precautionary measures. Be extremely careful when the surf is high.

If you get caught in a rip current, don't swim *against* it; swim *across* it, parallel to the shore. These currents, running from the shore out to sea, can often be spotted by their ragged-looking surface water and foamy edges.

Around coral reefs, wear something to protect your feet against coral cuts. Particularly good are the inexpensive Japanese *tabis*, or reef slippers. If you do sustain a coral cut, clean it with hydrogen peroxide, then apply an antiseptic or antibiotic substance. This is also a good procedure for octopus bites.

When stung by a Portuguese man-of-war or a jellyfish, mix unseasoned meat tenderizer with alcohol, leave it on the sting for ten or twenty minutes, then rinse it off with alcohol. The old Hawaiian remedies, which are reputedly quite effective, involve applying urine or green papaya.

If you step on the sharp, painful spines of a sea urchin, soak the affected area in very hot water for fifteen to ninety minutes. Another remedy calls for applying urine or undiluted

SHELL HUNTING

With over 1,500 varieties of shells washing up on its beaches, Hawaii has some of the world's finest shelling. The miles of sandy beach in Honolulu and around Oahu are prime areas for handpicking free souvenirs. Along the shores are countless shell specimens with names like horned helmet, Hebrew cone, Hawaiian olive, and Episcopal miter. Or you might find glass balls from Japan and sunbleached driftwood.

Beachcombing is the easiest method of shell gathering. Take along a small container and stroll through the backwash of the waves, watching for ripples from shells lying under the sand. You can also dive in shallow water where the ocean's surge will uncover shells.

It's tempting to walk along the top of coral reefs seeking shells and other marine souvenirs, but these living formations maintain a delicate ecological balance. Reefs in Hawaii and all over the planet are dying because of such plunder. In order to protect this underwater world, try to collect only shells and souvenirs that are adrift on the beach and no longer necessary to the marine ecology.

vinegar. If any of these preliminary treatments do not work, consult a doctor.

Oh, one last thing. The chances of encountering a shark are about as likely as sighting a UFO. But should you meet one of these ominous creatures, stay calm. He'll be no happier to see you than you are to confront him. Simply swim quietly to shore. By the time you make it back to terra firma, you'll have one hell of a story to tell.

SURFING

Oahu possesses some of the finest surfing breaks in the world. There are international contests here every year. For more information on both the participatory and spectator aspects of Oahu's surfing, contact the **Haleiwa Surf Center** (Haleiwa-Alii Beach Park, Haleiwa; 637-5051), or check out the island's many surf shops. Several stores in different parts of the island sell and rent boards: **Surf Line Hawaii** (508 Piikoi Street, Honolulu; 538-6911), **Downing Hawaii** (3021 Waialae Avenue, Honolulu; 737-9696), and **Hawaiian Island Creations** (354 Hahani Street, Kailua; 262-7277).

If you'd like to surf Waikiki, you can rent a board from **DeRussy Beach Service** (537-3717) on Fort DeRussy Beach, **Waikiki Beach Services** (in front of the Cinerama Reef Hotel), the **Outrigger Beachboy Service** (in front of the Outrigger Hotel), and the **Aloha Beach Service** (located near the Surfrider and Sheraton-Waikiki). Most of these outfits also provide lessons. If you are interested in learning to surf, Waikiki is an excellent place. The surf is gentle, but varied enough that you can move to more challenging spots as you gain proficiency. And there are many savvy, patient instructors among the "beach boys" here.

SKIN DIVING AND SCUBA DIVING

The following shops rent and sell equipment; they also offer lessons and underwater tours: **South Seas Aquatics** (1125 Ala Moana Boulevard, Honolulu; 538-3854), **Aloha Dive Shop** (Koko Marina Shopping Center, 7192 Kalanianaole Highway, Hawaii Kai; 395-5922), and **Aaron's Dive Shop** (39 Maluniu Avenue, Kailua; 261-1211).

The **Haleiwa Surf Center** (Haleiwa-Alii Beach Park, Haleiwa; 637-5051) teaches snorkeling, scuba diving, surfing, swimming, lifesaving, windsurfing, and sailing. This county agency is also an excellent source of information on island water sports and facilities.

SAILING

Hawaiiana Yacht Charters and Sailing Academy (1125 Ala Moana Boulevard, Honolulu; 521-6305) and **Islander Safaris** (1946 Young Street #320, Honolulu; 955-2202) sponsor sailboat cruises. The former is also an excellent place to charter sailboats.

WATERSKIING

Several organizations offer waterski outings for everyone from beginner to expert. If interested, contact **Tropical Water Ski** (923-4434) or the **Water Ski Center** (395-3773).

WINDSURFING

This young sport has gained increasing popularity throughout the islands. Enthusiasts take a surfboard, attach a sail, and set off fast as a trade wind across the ocean surface. If you'd like to try it, **Aloha Windsurfing** (926-1185) and **Windsurfing Tours Hawaii** (732-2721) rent equipment, provide lessons, and sponsor tours.

THE BEACH BUS

This public conveyance, which runs on weekends and holidays, is very convenient for aquatic enthusiasts. Leaving every hour, it runs from Monsarrat Avenue near the Kapiolani Park Bandstand to Hanauma Bay Beach Park, Sandy Beach, and Makapuu Beach Park. Surfboards are permitted.

GOLF AND TENNIS

What more could a golf or tennis player ask than a climate that's warm and sunny year-round? Nothing, of course, other than beautiful links and well-kept courts. Honolulu happens to have them all.

Golfers will remember that the Hawaiian Open is played here every year, and that the course on which the pros vie is only one of several outstanding facilities surrounding the city. In a region as lush and tropical as Honolulu it would be downright difficult to design a course that was *not* challenging and attractive. There are stately palms to line each fairway, enough sand to keep even Jack Nicklaus in trouble, and an oceanfront that makes Pebble Beach look like a driving range.

As a result, Oahu boasts about two dozen golf courses, more than half of which are open to the public. Tennis courts are even more plentiful. Many major hotels feature their own courts; in some cases these are for visitors use only, but oftentimes they are available to non-guests. There are also public courts galore, many equipped with lights for night play. But remember, the balmy weather and beautiful surroundings make tennis an extremely popular sport in these parts, so it is advisable to play on weekdays or else expect to wait for a court.

GOLF

You might consider any of the following courses—**Ala Wai Golf Course** (Honolulu; 737-3066), **Hawaii Kai Championship** (Honolulu; 395-2358); **Mililani Golf Club** (Mililani; 623-2254), **Olomana Golf Links** (Waimanalo; 259-7926), **Bay View Golf Center** (Kaneohe; 247-0451), **Pali Golf Course** (Kaneohe; 261-5853), **Kahuku Golf Course** (Kahuku; 293-5842), **Kuilima Hyatt Resort** (Kahuku; 293-8811), **Hawaii Country Club** (Aiea; 622-1744), **Ted Makalena Golf Course** (Waipahu; 671-0021), and **Makaha East** and **Makaha West Golf Courses** (Waianae; 695-9578).

TENNIS

In Honolulu there are courts at the following locations — **Ala Moana Park** (1201 Ala Moana Boulevard), **Hawaiian Regent Hotel** (2552 Kalakua Avenue; 922-6611), **Ilikai Hotel** (1777 Ala Moana Boulevard; 949-3811), **Iolani Tennis School** (563 Kamoku Street; 941-9555), **Kapiolani Tennis Courts** (2748 Kalakaua Avenue), and **King Street Courts** (2200 South King Street; 947-2625).

Outside Honolulu tennis facilities are located all around the island of Oahu. These include courts at **Hyatt Kuilima Resort** (Kahuku; 293-8811), **Koko Head District Park** (Hawaii Kai), and **Windward Tennis Club** (Kailua; 262-8834).

Since this is only a partial list, you can call the **County Department of Parks and Recreation** (523-4525) for further information on public courts, or the **Hawaii Visitors Bureau** (923-1811) to learn more about private courts available to the public.

RUNNING

If you happen to be a runner, you'll never lack for company in Honolulu. Hawaii reputedly has more joggers per capita than any place in the world. The sport is so popular that every year the capital city sponsors the Honolulu Marathon, generally considered one of the nation's top three marathon events.

As with other outdoor sports, Honolulu's tropical setting and salubrious climate make for ideal running conditions. There's a scent of wild fruit and salt spray in the air, and a flowering terrain that's backdropped by sheer mountain peaks. As a result, any time day or night you're likely to see legions of health-minded folks striding about town, putting in their daily exercise time.

Since this *is* Hawaii, runners, like everything else here, are as varied as a rainbow. Hawaiians, Japanese, Caucasians, Chinese, Filipinos, Samoans, and Portuguese alike don jogging shorts and shoes, then set off down cinder tracks, mountain trails, and beachfront paths.

Everyone's favorite run seems to be along the perimeter of **Kapiolani Park**. Featuring a flat, smooth surface, the course carries for 2.2 miles through Honolulu's most luxurious park and around the city zoo.

There's also a 4.6 mile run around **Diamond Head Crater**. The surface near this fabled landmark is relatively smooth, but there are some hills en route. Like the preceding course, it begins at the bandstand in Kapiolani Park.

Where else but Honolulu can you run circles around not one, but two volcanoes? **Punchbowl Crater**, in whose maw rests a National Memorial Cemetery, is encircled by a two-mile loop of residential streets which forms an excellent route.

Ala Moana Park's two-mile circumference makes for a lovely oceanfront jog. The course is flat and smooth, and the park itself quite alluring.

Another popular run leads through Honolulu's verdant **Manoa Valley** past the University of Hawaii campus. This figure-8 course can be taken in its entirety for 6.5 miles or run as a single 3.2 mile loop.

Two other courses go past spectacularly scenic areas. The **Tantalus-Roundtop**, a tough 10.1 miles through hilly terrain, provides outstanding vistas overlooking Honolulu. And the **Nuuanu Pali** run leads through 8.6 miles of intermittent hills, while affording equally dramatic views.

For further information on running in, through, and around the city, contact the **Honolulu Marathon Association** (3435 Waialae Avenue, Room 208; 734-7200). For equipment, you'll do well to stop by **The Running Room** (559 Kapahulu Avenue; 737-2422) or **Runner's Mart** (1246 South King Street; 531-7058). There's also a handy booklet available: "Runner's Guide" describes in detail the routes mentioned above and contains other information concerning Honolulu running.

Camping and Hiking

Camping on Oahu usually means pitching a tent or renting a camper. Throughout the island there are secluded spots and hidden beaches, plus numerous county and state parks. All these campsites, together with hiking trails, are described below; it's a good idea to consult those listings when planning your trip. You might also want to obtain U.S. Geological Survey maps, available from Hawaii Geographic Society, 217 South King Street, Suite 208, Honolulu, Oahu, HI 96817 (538-3952). The camping equipment you'll require is listed in a preceding chapter.

Before you set out, there are a few important matters I want to explain more fully. First, bring a campstove; firewood is scarce in most areas and soaking wet in others. It's advisable to wear long pants when hiking in order to protect your legs from rock outcroppings and spiny plants.

Most trails you'll be hiking are composed of volcanic rock. Since this is a very crumbly substance, be extremely cautious when climbing rock faces. In fact, you should avoid steep climbs if possible. Stay on the trails; Hawaii's dense undergrowth makes it very easy to get lost. If you get lost at night, stay where you are. Because of the low latitude, night descends rapidly here; there's practically no twilight. Once darkness falls, it can be very dangerous to move around. You should also be careful to purify all drinking water. And be extremely cautious near streambeds as flash-flooding sometimes occurs, particularly on the Windward Coast.

Another problem that you're actually more likely to encounter are those nasty varmints that buzz your ear just as you're falling asleep — mosquitoes. Hawaii contains neither poison ivy, but it has plenty of these dive-bombing pests. Like me, you probably consider that it's always open season on the bloody critters.

With most of the archipelago's other species, however, you'll have to be a careful conservationist. You'll be sharing the wilderness with pigs, goats, tropical birds, deer, and mongooses, as well as a spectacular array of exotic plants. They exist in one of the world's most delicate ecological balances. There are more endangered species in Hawaii than in all the rest of the United States. So keep in mind the maxim that the Hawaiians try to follow. *Ua mau ke ea o ka aina i ka pono:* The life of the land is preserved in righteousness.

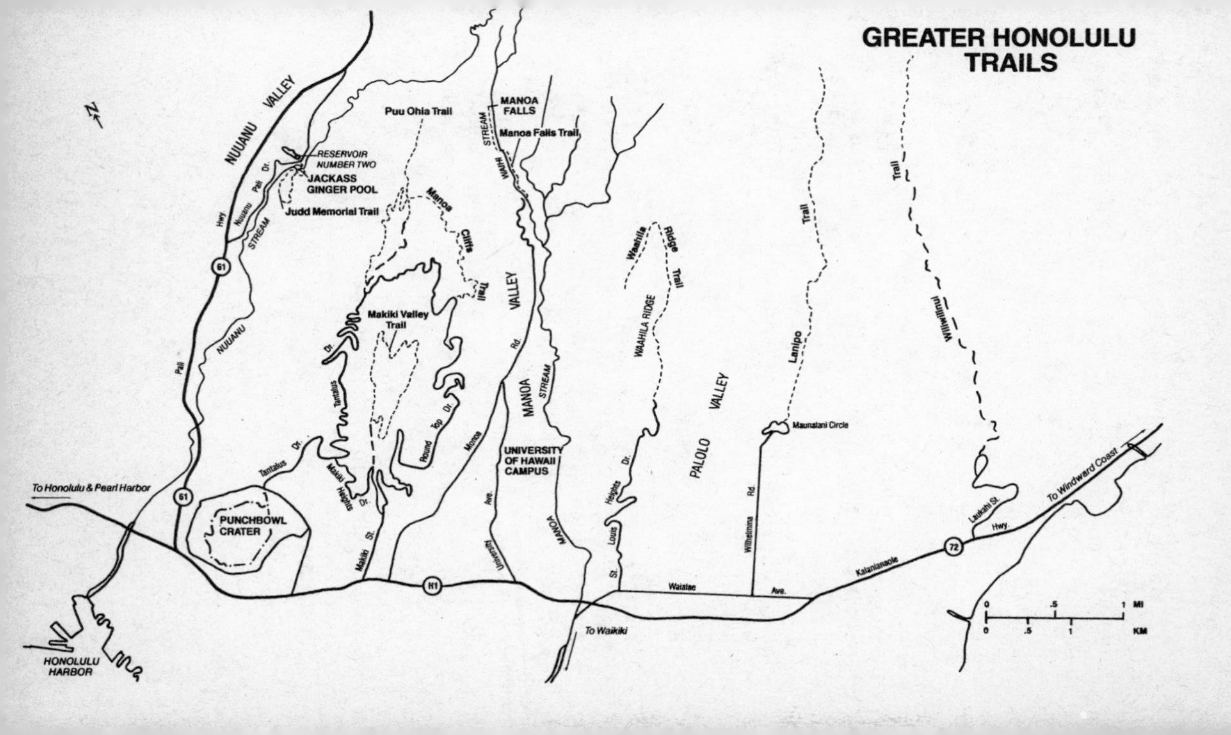
GREATER HONOLULU TRAILS
NUUANU VALLEY
Puu Ohia Trail
MANOA FALLS
STREAM
Manoa Falls Trail
WAIHI
RESERVOIR NUMBER TWO
JACKASS GINGER POOL
Judd Memorial Trail
Hwy
Nuuanu
Pali
Dr.
STREAM
61
Manoa Cliffs Trail
VALLEY
Waahila Ridge Trail
WAAHILA RIDGE
Lanipo Trail
Wiliwilinui Trail
Makiki Valley Trail
NUUANU
Pali
Tantalus Dr.
Round Top Dr.
Rd.
MANOA
STREAM
PALOLO VALLEY
Maunalani Circle
Manoa
UNIVERSITY OF HAWAII CAMPUS
Makiki Heights Dr.
Tantalus Dr.
Heights Dr.
Wilhelmina Rd.
Laukahi St.
To Windward Coast
To Honolulu & Pearl Harbor
61
PUNCHBOWL CRATER
Makiki St.
Ave.
University
MANOA
Louis St.
Hwy.
72
Kalanianaole
H1
Waialae Ave.
To Waikiki
HONOLULU HARBOR
0 .5 1 MI
0 .5 1 KM

CAMPING

There is only one campground in the city of Honolulu (described below under "Beaches and Parks"); those outside the city are listed in the "Beaches and Parks" section of the next chapter. Oahu has numerous overnight facilities, but as they are sometimes crowded, it's best to plan outdoor adventures far in advance and to schedule them for weekdays if possible.

Camping at **county parks** requires a permit which must be obtained two weeks in advance. These are issued free for a maximum of seven days, and are obtained from the Department of Parks and Recreation, Honolulu Municipal Building, 650 South King Street, Honolulu, Oahu, HI 96813 (523-4525) or at any of the "satellite city halls" around the island.

State park permits are free. They allow camping for seven days and must be obtained two weeks in advance. They are issued by the Division of State Parks, 1151 Punchbowl Street, Room 310, Honolulu, Oahu, HI 96813 (548-7455).

Remember when planning your trip, rainfall is heaviest on the Windward or East Coast, a little lighter on the North Shore, and lightest of all on the West Coast.

For camping equipment, check with **Omar The Tent Man**. Located at 1336 Dillingham Boulevard in Honolulu (841-0257), Omar rents and sells supplies. The following Honolulu sporting goods stores also sell gear: **The Great Outdoors** (98-019 Kamehameha Highway; 487-3615), **Honsport** (Ala Moana Center, 1450 Ala Moana Boulevard; 949-5591), and **Athletes Hawaii** (Ward Warehouse, 1050 Ala Moana Boulevard; 521-7152). Honsport also has a store out in Kailua (Kailua Shopping Center, Kailua Road).

Renting a camper is another excellent way to explore Oahu's countryside; you can travel turtle-like, with your shelter on your back. **Beach Boy Campers** (1720 Ala Moana Boulevard, Honolulu; 955-6381) has models starting at $31 a day, 3¢ a mile.

HIKING

There are numerous hiking trails within easy driving distance of Honolulu. Those in the greater Honolulu area are listed here; trails in other parts of the island are discussed in the next chapter. Unfortunately, many Oahu treks require special permission from the state, the armed services, or from private owners. But you should find that the hikes suggested, none of which require official sanction, will provide ample adventure.

To hike with a group or to obtain further information on hiking Oahu, contact the **Sierra Club** (1212 University Avenue, Honolulu, Oahu HI 96826; 946-8494) or the **Hawaii Audubon Society** (P.O. Box 22832, Honolulu, Oahu, HI 96822). Both agencies sponsor hikes regularly.

If you're staying in Waikiki, the most easily accessible hike is the short jaunt up **Diamond Head** crater. There's a sweeping view of Honolulu from atop this famous landmark. The trail begins inside the crater, so take Diamond Head Road around to the inland side of Diamond Head, then follow the tunnel leading into the crater.

In the Koolau Mountains above Diamond Head there are two parallel trails which climb almost 2,000 feet and afford excellent views of the Windward Coast. The head of **Wiliwilinui Trail** (3 miles long) can be reached by taking the Kalanianaole Highway (Routes H-1 and 72) east past the Kahala Mall Shopping Center. Then turn left on Laukahi Street and follow it a couple of miles to the top of the road. To get to **Lanipo Trail** (3 miles), located to the west of Wiliwilinui, take Waialae Avenue off Route H-1. Then turn up Wilhelmina Road and follow it to Maunalani Circle and the trailhead.

For spectacular views of the lush Palolo and Manoa Valleys, you can hike **Waahila Ridge Trail** (2 miles). To get there take St. Louis Heights Drive (near the University of Hawaii campus) and then follow connecting roads up to Waahila Ridge State Recreation Area.

Another hike, along **Manoa Falls Trail** (0.8 mile), leads right through the valley. This is a pleasant jaunt which follows Waihi Stream through a densely vegetated area to a charming waterfall.

Manoa Cliffs Trail (3 miles), a pleasant family hike, follows a precipice along the west side of Manoa Valley. And **Puu Ohia Trail** (2 miles), which crosses Manoa Cliffs Trail, provides splendid views of Manoa and Nuuanu Valleys. Both trails begin from Tantalus Drive in the hills above Honolulu.

Makiki Valley Trail (2 miles) begins near Tantalus Drive. Composed of three interlinking trails, this loop passes stands of eucalyptus and bamboo trees and offers some sweeping views of Honolulu.

Another loop trail, **Judd Memorial** (1.3 mile), crosses Nuuanu Stream and traverses bamboo, eucalyptus, and Norfolk pine groves en route to the Jackass Ginger Pool. This is a marvelous place to swim, and, if you've tried some of the nearby mud-sliding chutes, to wash off as well. To get there, take the Pali Highway (Route 61) several miles north from Honolulu. Turn onto Nuuanu Pali Drive and follow it about a mile to Reservoir Number Two spillway.

In the mountains above Pearl Harbor, at Keaiwa Heiau State Park, you'll find the **Aiea Loop Trail** (4.8 miles). Set in a heavily forested area, this hike passes the wreckage of a World War II cargo plane. It provides an excellent chance to see some of the native trees—*lehua, ohia*, and *koa*—used by local woodworkers. (For directions to the state park, see the "Beaches and Parks" section in the following chapter.)

Another hike in this general area, along **Waimano Trail** (7 miles), climbs 1,600 feet to an astonishing vista point above Oahu's Windward Coast. There are swimming holes en route. To get there take Kamehameha Highway (Route 90) west to Waimano Home Road (Route 730). Turn right and go two-and-a-half miles to a point along the road where you'll see a building on the right and an irrigation ditch on the left. The trail follows the ditch.

Fishing and Gathering

Fishing in Hawaii is good all year round, and the offshore waters are crowded with many varieties of edible fish. For deep-sea fishing you'll have to charter a boat, and fresh-water angling requires a license; so most visitors concentrate on surf-casting. It involves little expense or preparation.

The easiest way to fish is with a hand-held line. Just get a fifty- to one-hundred-foot line, and attach a hook and a ten-ounce sinker. Wind the line loosely around a smooth block of wood, then remove the wood from the center. If your coil is free from snags, you'll be able to throw-cast it easily. You can either hold the line in your hand, feeling for a strike, or tie it to the frail end of a bamboo pole.

Beaches and rocky points are generally good places to surf-cast; the best times are during the incoming and outgoing tides. Popular baits include octopus, eel, lobster, crab, frozen shrimp, and sea worms. You can also fish with lures. The ancient Hawaiians used pearl shells to attract the fish, and hooks, some made from human bones, to snare them. Your friends will probably be quite content to see you angling with store-bought artificial lures.

If you want to buy or rent more sophisticated tackle, there are numerous shops in Honolulu. For information on seasons, licenses, and official regulations, check with the **Fish and Game Division** of the State Department of Land and Natural Resources (1151 Punchbowl; 548-4002). For deep-sea fishing, contact **Coreene-C Sport Fishing Charters** (536-7472) or **Island Charters** (536-1555), both docked in Honolulu's Kewalo Basin.

TORCHFISHING AND SPEARFISHING

The old Hawaiians also fished at night by torchlight. They fashioned torches by inserting nuts from the *kukui* tree into the hollow end of a bamboo pole, then lighting the flammable nuts. When fish swam like moths to the flame, the Hawaiians speared, clubbed, or netted them.

The best time to find local people torchfishing is a dark night when the sea is calm and the tide low. During daylight hours, you might discover folks spearfishing along coral reefs and in areas where the bottom is a mixture of sand and rock.

CRABBING

For local crab hunters, there are two important crab species in Hawaii—Kona crabs and Samoan crabs. The Kona variety are found in relatively deep water, and can usually be caught only from a boat. Samoan crabs inhabit sandy and muddy areas in bays and near river mouths. All that's needed to catch them is a net fastened to a round wire hoop and secured by a string. The net is lowered to the bottom; then, after a crab has gone for the bait, the entire contraption is raised to the surface.

SQUIDDING

Between June and December, squidding is another popular sport. Actually, the term is a misnomer; squid inhabit deep water and are not usually hunted. What squidders will really be after are octopuses. There are two varieties in Hawaii, both of which are commonly found in water three or four feet deep:

the *hee*, a greyish-brown animal which changes color like a chameleon, and the *puloa*, a red-colored mollusk with white stripes on its head.

Both are nocturnal and live in the holes along coral reefs. At night by torchlight they can be seen sitting exposed on the bottom. During the day, they crawl inside the holes, covering the entrances with shells and loose coral.

The Hawaiians used to pick the octopus up, letting it cling to their chest and shoulders. When they were ready to bag their prize, they'd dispatch the creature by biting it between the eyes. Beginners usually feel more comfortable spearing the beast.

SHELLFISH GATHERING

Another popular sport involves collecting the shellfish that inhabit coastal waters. Oysters and clams, which use their muscular feet to burrow into sand and soft mud, can be gathered along the bottom of Hawaii's bays. Lobsters, though illegal to spear, can be taken with short poles to which cable leaders and baited hooks are attached. It's also possible to take limpets, though I don't recommend it. These tiny black shellfish, locally known as *opihi*, cling tenaciously to rocks in areas of very rough surf. The Hawaiians gather them by leaping into the water after one set of waves breaks, then jumping out before the next set arrives. Being a coward myself, I simply order them in Hawaiian restaurants.

SEAWEED GATHERING

Few people think of seaweed as food, but it's very popular today among the Japanese, and it once served as an integral part of the Hawaiian diet. It's extremely nutritious, easy to gather, and very plentiful.

Rocky shores are the best places to find the edible species of seaweed. Some of them float in to shore and can be picked up; other species cling stubbornly to rocks and must be freed with a knife; still others grow in sand or mud. Low tide is the best time to collect seaweed; more plants are exposed, and some can be taken without even getting wet.

Picking Fruit

There's a lot more to Hawaii's tropical wonderland than gorgeous flowers and overgrown rain forests. The islands are also teeming with edible plants. Roots, fruits, vegetables, herbs, and spices grow like weeds from the shoreline to the mountains. Here's a brief list of some of the islands' more common fruits. They can be picked by hand, poked with a stick, or plucked with a fruit-picker.

Banana: The Polynesians once used banana trees not only for food, but also for clothing, roofing, medicines, dyes, and even alcohol. The fruit, which grows upside-down on broad-leaved trees, can be harvested as soon as the first banana in the bunch turns yellow.

Coconut: The coconut tree is probably the most important plant in the entire Pacific. Every part of the towering palm is used. You'll probably be concerned only with the hard brown nut, which yields delicious milk as well as a tasty meat.

Climbing a coconut palm is a task for the daring or foolhardy; personally, I wait for the nuts to fall and then pick them up off the ground. If the coconut is still green, the meat is a succulent jelly-like substance. Otherwise it's a hard but delicious white rind.

Papaya: These delicious fruits, which are picked as they begin to turn yellow, grow on unbranched trees. Summer is the peak harvesting season.

Guava: Roundish yellow fruits which grow on a small shrub or tree, these are extremely abundant in the wild. They ripen between June and October.

Mango: Known as the king of fruits, the mango grows on tall shade trees. The oblong fruit ripens in the spring and summer.

Breadfruit: These large round fruits grow on trees that reach up to sixty feet high. Breadfruit must be boiled, baked, or fried.

Mountain apple: This sweet fruit grows in damp, shaded valleys at an elevation of about 1,800 feet. The flowers resemble fluffy crimson balls; the fruit, which ripens from July to December, is also a rich red color.

Passion fruit: This delicious yellow fruit, oval in shape, grows to a length of about two or three inches. It's produced on a vine and ripens in summer or fall.

Avocado: Covered with a tough green or purple skin, this pear-shaped fruit sometimes weighs as much as three pounds. It grows on ten- to forty-foot-high trees, and ripens from June through November.

Beaches and Parks

WAIKIKI BEACH

With its sparkling swath of white sand, Waikiki numbers among the world's foremost beaches. To most people it is a sandy ribbon two miles long, which extends from the foot of Diamond Head to the Ala Wai Canal and marks the seaside boundary of Honolulu's Waikiki district. But to local folks, Waikiki is many beaches in one: each section of this sun-drenched corridor has a name, a tradition, and a personal ambience. When you park your beach towel here, or stroll the shoreline, consider that every few strides will carry you into another realm of Honolulu's culture and history.

Sans Souci, in the shadow of Diamond Head, runs from the New Otani Kaimana Beach Hotel to the Natatorium. Back in the 1880s, it was a favorite haunt of Robert Louis Stevenson. Today it's an appealing retreat for those seeking sun and sand in Waikiki's quiet corner.

Kapiolani Beach Park, across the street from the park's intricately landscaped grounds, is quite an intriguing place. The Natatorium, marking one end of the beach, was built in the '20s as a World War I memorial and is the world's largest saltwater swimming pool.

The sandy area nearby is **Queen's Surf**, which offers bathroom, shower, and informal dining facilities. This is the bohemian quarter of Waikiki, attracting local artists, gays, conga drummers, and a plethora of fascinating characters. The beach is particularly colorful on weekends.

Kuhio Beach Park reaches from Kapahulu Avenue to Kaiulani Avenue. Here, in addition to a broad sandy white beach, you'll find numerous facilities—bathhouses, surfboard rentals, lifeguard stands, and shady pavilions that draw local card players and chess masters. Some of Waikiki's best budget restaurants are located right across the street. Because of these excellent facilities and the beach's central location, it's usually quite crowded. People watchers find it a great place to check out locals and tourists alike; and for parents, there's a protective seawall that provides a safe area to take children swimming.

Royal-Moana Beach is in the heart of Waikiki. Stretching between Waikiki's oldest hotels, the Moana and the Royal Hawaiian, it has traditionally been the gathering place for beachgoers. Today is no different: in addition to the two grande dames, there are other major hotels, offering beachfront bars and restaurants. There are also stands renting surfboards and umbrellas; just offshore "Queen's Surf" and "Canoe's Surf," Waikiki's most famous breaks, await the surfboard enthusiast.

Fort DeRussy Beach, owned by the military but open to the public, features the area's widest swath of beach. This beautiful strand is an excellent spot for sunbathing. It also offers beach rental facilities and easy access to restaurants and shops.

Nearby **Kahanamoku Beach**, wedged between the ocean and a shallow lagoon, marks the *ewa* edge of Waikiki Beach. Named for Hawaii's great surfer, Duke Kahanamoku, the beach fronts the Hilton Hawaiian Village and is close to numerous facilities.

For **Waikiki Beach** in its entirety, you can follow these guidelines.

Facilities: Picnic areas, restrooms, showers, concession stands, recreation buildings, lifeguards, aquarium, and beach equipment rentals. There are oceanfront bars and restaurants; you'll find numerous markets and shops nearby.

Camping: Not permitted.

Swimming: Very good; most of the area is protected by a coral reef.

Snorkeling: Fair.

Surfing: This is a prime beach for surfing; the wave action is particularly good for beginners, but experts also frequent Waikiki when the waves are larger.

Fishing: The beach is often too crowded for fishing; should you find a secluded spot, look for *papio, moano*, goatfish, and bonefish.

Getting there: Waikiki Beach parallels Kalakaua Avenue and Ala Moana Boulevard from the Sans Souci area to the Ala Wai Canal.

GREATER HONOLULU BEACHES AND PARKS

Ala Moana Beach Park—Located directly across from Ala Moana Center, this seventy-six-acre park is a favorite with Hawaii residents. On weekends every type of outdoor enthusiast imaginable turns out to swim, fish, jog, fly model airplanes, sail model boats, and so on. There's a curving length of beach, a grassy park area, recreation facilities galore, and a lot of local color.

Facilities: Picnic area, restrooms, showers, concession stands, tennis courts, recreation building, bowling green, and lifeguards. Markets and restaurants are nearby.

Camping: Not permitted.

Swimming: Good.

Snorkeling: Fair.

Surfing: There are three separate breaks here. "Concessions," "Tennis Courts," and "Baby Haleiwa" all have summer waves.

Fishing: The most common catches are *papio,* bonefish, goatfish, and *moano.*

Getting there: Located on Ala Moana Boulevard at the west end of Waikiki, across from Ala Moana Center.

Sand Island State Park—This 140-acre park wraps around the south and east shores of Sand Island, with sections fronting both Honolulu Harbor and the open sea. Despite the name, there's no sandy beach here, and jet traffic from nearby Honolulu International might disturb your snoozing. But there is a great view of Honolulu. Open 6:30 a.m. to 7 p.m. daily.

Facilities: Restrooms and picnic area. Market and restaurants nearby.

Camping: State permit required for tent camping in the grassy area facing the ocean.

Swimming: Poor.

Snorkeling: Poor.

Surfing: Summer breaks.

Fishing: Bonefish, goatfish, *papio*, and *moano* are the prime catches.

Getting there: From Waikiki, take Ala Moana Boulevard and Nimitz Highway several miles west to Sand Island Access Road.

Diamond Head Beach Park—This twisting ribbon of white sand sits directly below the crater. It's close enough to Waikiki for convenient access but far enough to shake most of the crowds. The Kuilei cliffs, covered with scrub growth, loom behind the beach.

Facilities: Shower. It's about two miles to markets and restaurants in Waikiki.

Camping: None.

Swimming: Mediocre.

Snorkeling: Good. Coral reef extends offshore throughout this area.

Surfing: Year-round juice at "Lighthouse" breaks.

Fishing: Your chances are good to reel in *ulua, papio*, or *mamao.*

CHAPTER V

Beyond Honolulu

Enthralling as Honolulu can be, there is even more that awaits the visitor to Hawaii's capital. Just beyond the city's vibrant thoroughfares, stretching across the rest of Oahu, is an equally exciting realm. The island features countless beaches, plus two blade-steep mountain ranges. Since most of Oahu's residents live in the southern regions around Honolulu, the north is rural. To visitors this means you can experience the color and velocity of the city, then leisurely tour through enchanting countryside.

Major highways lead from the capital along the east and west coasts, and several roads bisect the central plateau en route to the North Shore. Except for a five-mile strip in Oahu's northwest corner, you can drive completely around the island.

Closest to Honolulu is the east coast, where a spectacular seascape is paralleled by the Koolaus, a jagged and dauntless mountain range. This is Oahu's rainswept Windward Coast. Here, traveling up the coast past the bedroom-communities of Kailua and Kaneohe, you'll discover beautiful and relatively untouched white-sand beaches. On the North Shore are some of the world's most famous surfing spots—Waimea Bay, Sunset, the Banzai Pipeline—where waves twenty and thirty feet high roll in with crushing force.

The Waianae Range, rising to 4,040 feet, shadows Oahu's western coast. The sands are as white here, the beaches as uncrowded, but there is sometimes more hostility to visitors. So I usually recommend that people touch lightly on this Leeward Coast, if at all, and concentrate their daytrips and overnighters around other parts of the island.

Between the Koolau and Waianae Ranges, remnants of the two volcanoes that created Oahu, spreads the Leilehua Pla-

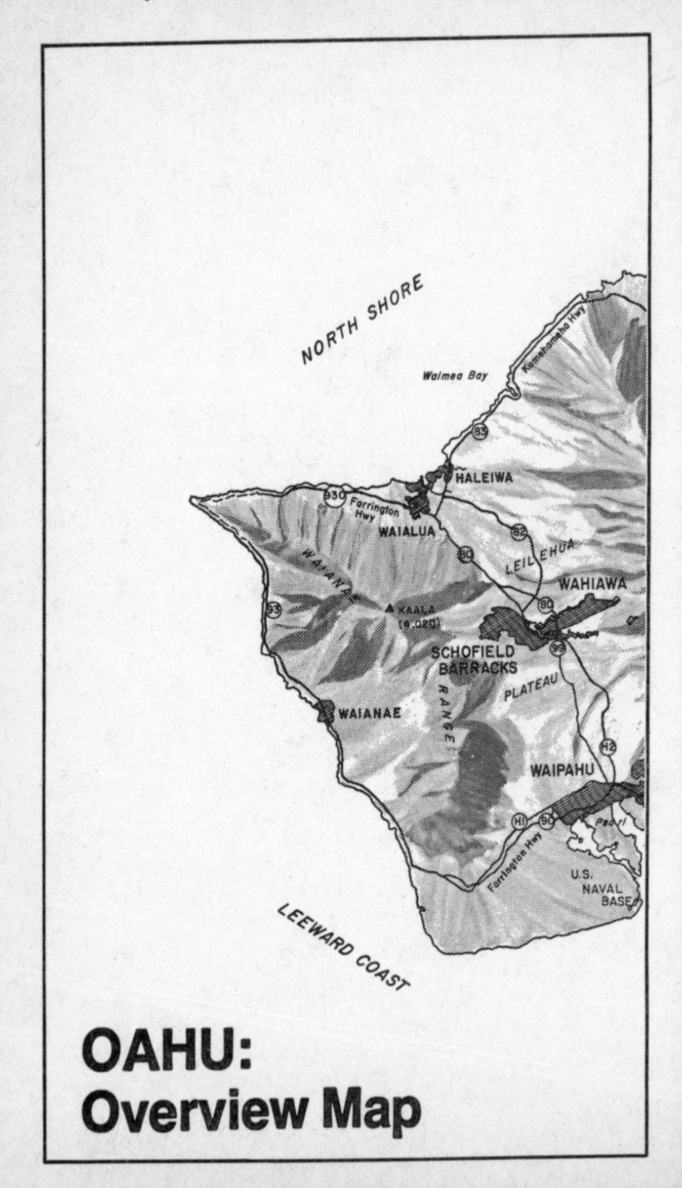
NORTH SHORE
Waimea Bay
Kamehameha Hwy
83
HALEIWA
930
Farrington Hwy
WAIALUA
82
80
LEILEHUA
WAHIAWA
80
93
KAALA
SCHOFIELD
BARRACKS
99
PLATEAU
RANGE
WAIANAE
H2
WAIPAHU
H1
90
Pearl
Farrington Hwy
U.S.
NAVAL
BASE
LEEWARD COAST
OAHU:
Overview Map

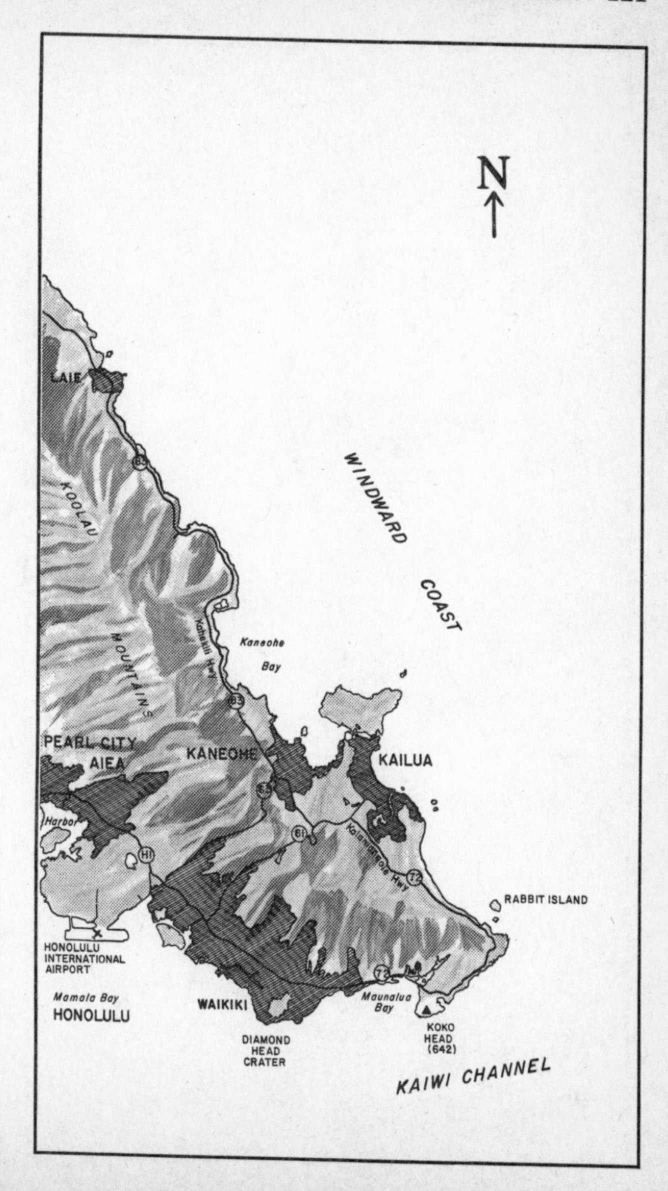
N
LAIE
KOOLAU
MOUNTAINS
WINDWARD
COAST
Kahekili Hwy
Kaneohe
Bay
PEARL CITY
AIEA
KANEOHE
KAILUA
Harbor
Kalanianaole Hwy
RABBIT ISLAND
HONOLULU
INTERNATIONAL
AIRPORT
Mamala Bay
HONOLULU
WAIKIKI
Maunalua
Bay
KOKO
HEAD
(642)
DIAMOND
HEAD
CRATER
KAIWI CHANNEL

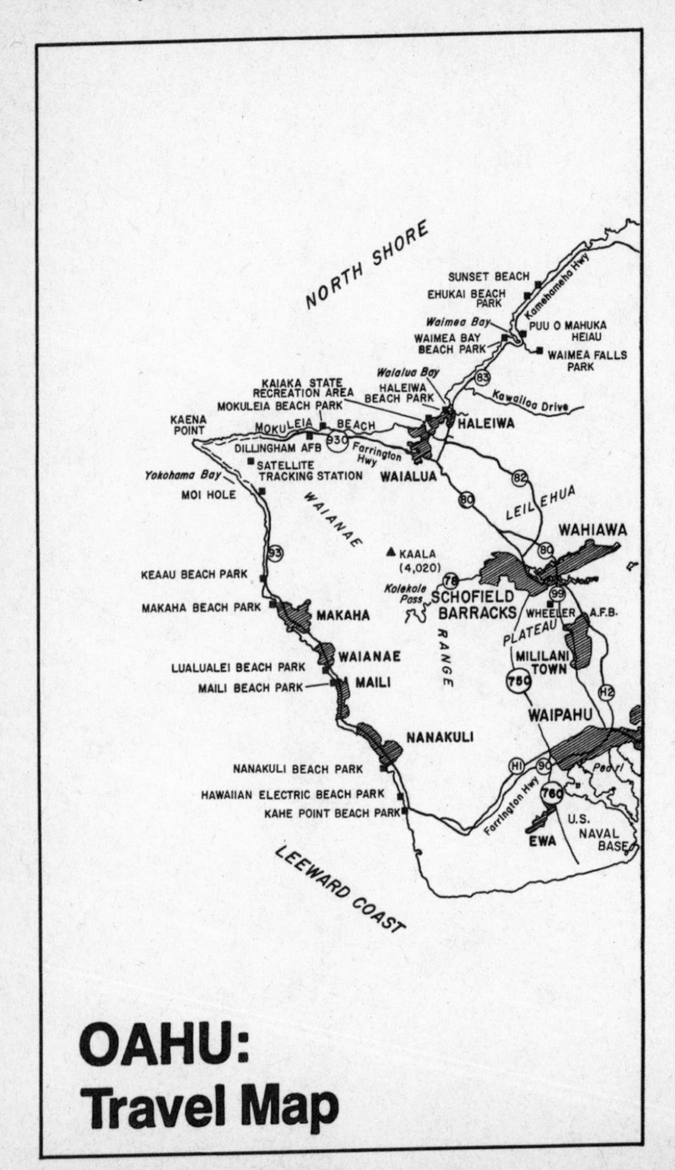

OAHU: Travel Map

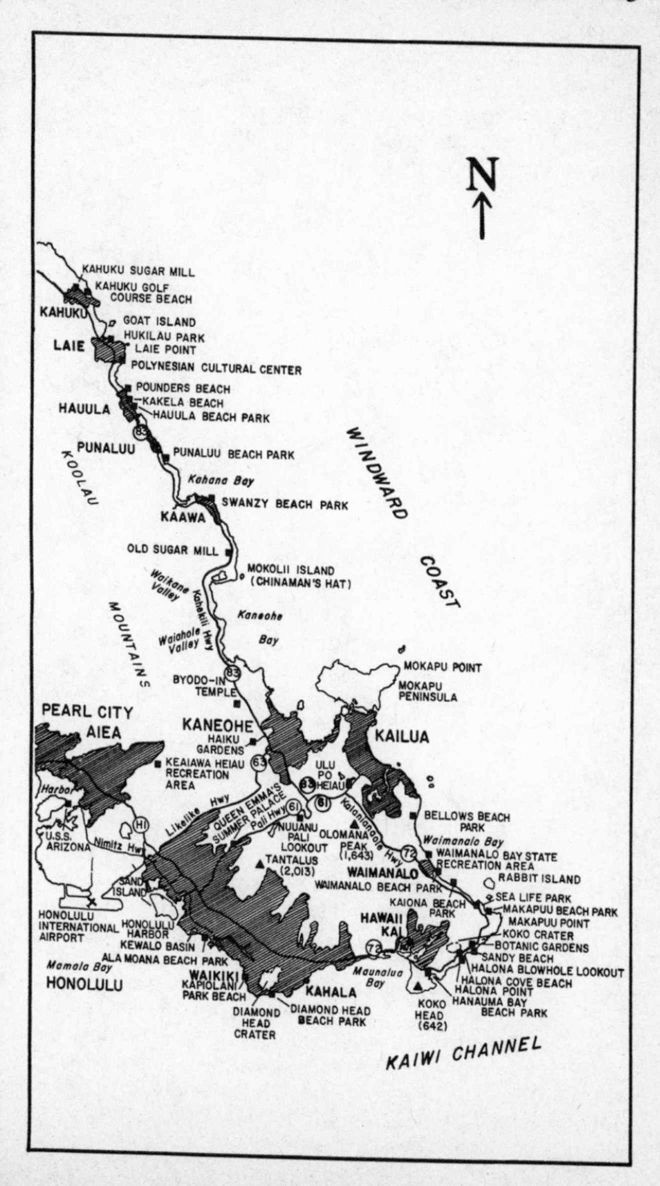
N
KAHUKU SUGAR MILL
KAHUKU GOLF COURSE BEACH
KAHUKU
GOAT ISLAND
HUKILAU PARK
LAIE
LAIE POINT
POLYNESIAN CULTURAL CENTER
POUNDERS BEACH
KAKELA BEACH
HAUULA
HAUULA BEACH PARK
PUNALUU
PUNALUU BEACH PARK
KOOLAU
Kahana Bay
SWANZY BEACH PARK
KAAWA
WINDWARD
OLD SUGAR MILL
MOKOLII ISLAND (CHINAMAN'S HAT)
COAST
Waikane Valley
Kahekili Hwy
MOUNTAINS
Kaneohe
Bay
Waiahole Valley
MOKAPU POINT
MOKAPU PENINSULA
BYODO-IN TEMPLE
PEARL CITY
AIEA
KANEOHE
KAILUA
HAIKU GARDENS
KEAIAWA HEIAU RECREATION AREA
ULU PO HEIAU
Harbor
Likelike Hwy
QUEEN EMMA'S SUMMER PALACE
Pali Hwy
Kalanianaole Hwy
BELLOWS BEACH PARK
U.S.S. ARIZONA
Nimitz Hwy
NUUANU PALI LOOKOUT
OLOMANA PEAK (1,643)
Waimanalo Bay
WAIMANALO BAY STATE RECREATION AREA
TANTALUS (2,013)
WAIMANALO
RABBIT ISLAND
SAND ISLAND
WAIMANALO BEACH PARK
SEA LIFE PARK
KAIONA BEACH PARK
MAKAPUU BEACH PARK
HONOLULU INTERNATIONAL AIRPORT
HONOLULU HARBOR
HAWAII KAI
MAKAPUU POINT
KOKO CRATER
KEWALO BASIN
BOTANIC GARDENS
ALA MOANA BEACH PARK
SANDY BEACH
Mamala Bay
WAIKIKI
Maunalua Bay
HALONA BLOWHOLE LOOKOUT
HONOLULU
KAPIOLANI PARK BEACH
KAHALA
HALONA COVE BEACH
HALONA POINT
HANAUMA BAY BEACH PARK
DIAMOND HEAD CRATER
DIAMOND HEAD BEACH PARK
KOKO HEAD (642)
KAIWI CHANNEL

teau. This fertile region is occupied by sugar and pineapple plantations, and hosts several military bases.

In the course of a day's drive, you can tour the entire island; but you might consider putting up at a rural hotel and spending a few relaxing days in the country. It could prove almost as much fun as Honolulu.

The Good Life

Hotels

Once outside the glow of Honolulu's city lights, you'll find the overnight accommodations few and scattered. But the rooms that are available range widely enough in price to fit any purse. Most of the facilities have a countrified atmosphere that makes them mighty homey. And several of the places, even by Honolulu's rigorous standards, are quite pleasant. So if you're looking to settle in outside town, you need look no farther than the following.

WINDWARD COAST HOTELS

If you don't mind funky living, check out the **Countryside Cabins** (53-224 Kamehameha Highway; 237-8169) in Punaluu. These old clapboard structures, complete with fading paint and linoleum floors, are set in beautiful garden surroundings across the street from the ocean. Depending on your taste, you'll find the one-room cottages either claustrophobic or quaint. But no one will find fault with the price ($10 double for a room without kitchenette, $14 with; $24 for a two-bedroom cottage), or with Margaret Naai, the charming Asian woman who runs this unique establishment.

Just down the road, but a world away, you'll find **Pat's At Punaluu** (53-567 Kamehameha Highway; 293-8111 or toll-free 800-252-0078), a 136-unit high-rise condo on the Punaluu beach. The one-bedroom "lodge" units come complete with lanai, kitchen, washer-dryer, and shower-tub combinations. Brick walls and carpeting create a pleasant atmosphere. Even cozier, however, are the four-plex cottages next to the beach, which rent for $40 and house up to four people. "Lodge" accommodations are $37 (rates lower during off-season). All rooms have an ocean view; the condo also contains a pool, sauna, and exercise room. Its excellent location and friendly staff make Pat's an outstanding choice.

The **Laniloa Lodge** (55-109 Laniloa Street, Laie; 293-9282) is a modern low-slung facility next to the Polynesian Cultural Center. A lot of tour buses roll into the center, detracting somewhat from the lodge's surroundings. But the rooms are nicely decorated and comfortable, though a bit antiseptic. They come with color televisions, air-conditioning, telephones, wall-to-wall carpeting, and shower-tub combinations. The rates ($29 single, $33 double) are less during the slow season.

NORTH SHORE HOTELS

The North Shore's bid for world-class status is the **Hyatt Kuilima Resort** (Kahuku; 293-8811). Situated midway round the island, it is far and away the plushest place you'll find outside Honolulu. The Hyatt is an 880-acre resort dramatically set on a peninsula and fringed by a white-sand beach. Matter of fact, you'd be hard pressed to find a better location for a hotel. With the sea at your doorstep and mountains backdropping the entire scene, it's overwhelming. Every room in this 487-room facility looks out either upon the ocean or one of the two bays that border the hotel. If that's not enough, there are tennis courts, riding trails, a surfside swimming pool, and a golf course. The rooms, happily, are equal to all this. They range from "bay view" facilities ($60 double; $50 from April to December) to high-elevation rooms with ocean vistas ($82 double; $72 off-season). Private cabanas spotted about the grounds are priced upward from $85 double.

The **Mokuleia Beach Colony** (68-615 Farrington Highway, Waialua; 637-9311) claims to be "Hawaii's best-kept secret." It's an ideal hideaway, located along a sandy beach on Oahu's rustic North Shore. The living is condo style in a colony of duplex cottages scattered across palm-studded grounds. Each unit is a spacious one-bedroom apartment with an enclosed lanai and all-electirc kitchen. The cottages are reasonably modern—they were built in the '60s—and combine shingle roofs with attractive wood trim. There's a pool and courts (tennis, paddle-tennis, and basketball) on the property, plus a polo field next door. Minimum stay is one week. Poolside cottages are $250 a week, beachfront accommodations $335. From December 15 to April 14, they increase to $335 and $365, respectively.

LEEWARD COAST HOTELS

There are three oceanfront condominiums along Oahu's western shore in Makaha. I was not impressed with any of them. Also, I feel the local hostility toward visitors makes this area undesirable. But I'll list the condos and let you decide for yourself.

Makaha Beach Cabanas (84-965 Farrington Highway; 696-2166 or toll-free 800-367-5205) has very small, attractive one-bedroom apartments for $35 double. There is a two-night minimum. This high-rise condo fronts a pretty white-sand beach.

Makaha Surfside (85-175 Farrington Highway; 695-9574) offers studios for $30 and one-bedroom units for $35. This sprawling facility fronts a rocky beach and has two swimming pools, a sauna, and a jogging path.

Makaha Shores Apartment Hotel (84-265 Farrington Highway; 696-7121), located next to a white-sand beach, offers studios for $140 a week, one-bedroom apartments for $210, and two-bedrooms for $280 (peak season rates from December to May are $210, $280, and $350, respectively). One week minimum stay.

Restaurants

As many fine dining establishments as Honolulu might have, the city certainly cannot claim a monopoly. You'll discover why when you set out along Oahu's rural coasts. There won't be an abundance of gourmet-class restaurants, but you'll doubtless enjoy several outstanding meals.

WINDWARD COAST RESTAURANTS

Spotted along Oahu's eastern shore are a number of moderately-priced restaurants which may prove handy if you're beachcombing or sightseeing. Most are located on or near Routes 72 (Kalanianaole Highway) and 83 (Kamehameha Highway), the adjoining roads leading from Honolulu along the coast. For the sake of convenience I'll list the restaurants as they will appear when you travel north.

The first, **Molly's** (7192 Kalanianaole Highway; 395-6229), a plain cafe in the Koko Marina Shopping Center, is convenient when you're at a beach in Oahu's beautiful southeast corner. The food is standard American fare, the portions are ample, the prices modest. Sandwiches run about $3. Hot meals—complete with soup or salad, french fries or rice, and beverage—are generally under $4.50.

For health foods, **House of Nutrition** (395-9166), in the same shopping complex, has a juice bar serving light vegetarian meals.

Farther north, **Waimanalo Snack Bar** (41-1029 Kalanianaole Highway; 259-9031) has sandwiches and plate lunches at greasy-spoon prices. No gourmet's delight, this tiny eatery is well-placed for people enjoying Waimanalo's beaches.

Kailua is a bedroom community with a splendid beach. Since you might find yourself nearby at lunchtime or when returning from the beach, I'll briefly describe a few restaurants. For crepes, quiche, or a light seafood dish, try **Bib's Family Restaurant** (315 Uluniu; 261-8724). **Island Health** (602 Kailua Road; 261-9461) has a snack bar in its health food store.

In Kaneohe, another suburban town next door, you might like **Eggs 'N' Things** (46-126 Kahuhipa Street; 235-5772). Though slightly overpriced, it's a tastefully appointed restaurant with a bill of fare that includes pancakes, waffles, crepes suzette, eggs, and things. Or, if you want to take a snack to the beach, check out **Fuji Delicatessen and Restaurant** (46-138 Kahuhipa Street; 235-5633) with its inexpensive sandwiches and Japanese plates.

You'll doubtless hear about **Crouching Lion Inn** (Kamehameha Highway, Kaawa; 237-8511). It's a classy, well-known restaurant overlooking the sea. I haven't eaten here, but the place has received bad reviews from friends.

For natural food, **Better Life Health Food Store** (Laie Shopping Center, 55-510 Kamehameha Highway, Laie; 293-9332) serves salads, smoothies, sandwiches, and tostadas.

There's one restaurant on the Windward Coast for those special occasions when elegance is more important than expense. That's **Pat's at Punaluu** (53-567 Kamehameha Highway; 293-8502). Wicker chairs, bamboo dividers, and a palm-studded patio create an inviting atmosphere; the view at this beachfront establishment adds to the tropic ambience. At dinner there's a surf-and-turf menu, priced from $9 to $14, which includes *kalua* pig, rack of lamb, steak, Cornish game hen, shrimp tempura, and the catch of the day. The seafood is exceptionally good, but I found the steak a little tough. Pat's lunch menu offers several salad and sandwich selections for about $4, plus shrimp curry, teriyaki steak, tempura, Hawaiian barbecued ribs, and other dishes tabbed between $4 and $6.

NORTH SHORE RESTAURANTS

The Hyatt Kuilima Resort, several miles north, features two excellent restaurants. At the **Garden Terrace** (293-8811), overlooking the hotel's lovely grounds, you'll encounter good dining in an attractive environment. The restaurant has a surf-and-turf menu which includes seafood crepes, steak, *mahimahi*, and teriyaki beef. There's also a sumptuous buffet at breakfast and dinner. Or, for a splurge meal, try **Jonah's Sea Catch** (293-8811). This gourmet establishment serves up lobster thermidor, scampi, and other special seafood dishes. Entrees run from about $16 to $19 and reservations are required, but the dress is casual.

When you're around Sunset Beach, **Aricia's Beach Inn Kitchen** (59-176 Kamehameha Highway; 638-8200) is quite convenient. It's a roadside take-out stand preparing natural foods. Here you can find soups, salads, sandwiches, smoothies, or Mexican dishes at low prices.

Otherwise the best place to chow down is in Haleiwa, the main town on the North Shore. My recommendation is **Sea View Inn** (corner of Kamehameha Highway and Haleiwa Road; 637-4165). This L-shaped cafe, with an adjoining lounge, has a mixed menu. There are a few fish dishes, several Chinese choices, fried liver, and a couple of beef platters, each around $3 to $5. Or you can pick up a sandwich for a buck or two.

Country Natural Foods (66-470 Kamehameha Highway; 637-9543) has a juice bar and snack shop.

And **Banzai Bowl** (66-200 Kamehameha Highway), a small Japanese restaurant, has an *okazu* counter from which you can select such finger foods as *sushi*, fish cakes, *lumpias*, etc.

Small town though it is, Haleiwa also has a little espresso house, **Da Cuppa Kope** (66-134 Kamehameha Highway; 637-6647). Being a hopeless caffeine addict, I always seem to end up here. But even if you're not a "caffiend," you might enjoy pulling up at the counter or sinking into a wicker chair and gathering in this local gathering place.

LEEWARD COAST RESTAURANTS

This sparsely populated strip of shoreline has several dining spots. All are located on Farrington Highway, the main road, and most are in the town of Waianae. Within a short distance of one another are **Cathay Inn Chop Suey** (86-088 Farrington Highway; 696-9477), a good choice for Chinese cuisine; **Masago's Restaurant** (86-032 Farrington Highway; 696-6137) for Japanese and Hawaiian food; and **Manila Delite Cafeteria** (85-888 Farrington Highway) for Filipino dishes.

Nearby **Smiley's Pizza Foundry** (85-773 Farrington Highway; 696-9676) operates from a tiny roadside stand, but the owners boast that they'll "make you a pizza you can't refuse." They might just be right; not only is the food delicious, it's cheap, too. In addition to pizzas, Smiley's also serves Mexican snacks for about a buck and sandwiches for two bucks.

If you'd like something with more class, there's the **Rusty Harpoon** (87-064 Farrington Highway; 696-6345) in Maili. It's an attractive open-air restaurant with a balcony overlooking the ocean. Ceiling fans, captains' chairs, and nautical lamps lend charm to this restaurant. The lunch menu features salads and sandwiches from $3 to $5, and specialty platters (*mahimahi,* chopped steak, barbecued ribs, etc.) for slightly more. At dinnertime the menu rises sharply into the $9 to $14 range with prime rib, fried chicken teriyaki, *mahimahi,* shrimp tempura, and other seafood dishes.

Grocery Markets

Once outside Honolulu, there are grocery markets all along the Windward Coast. Many are listed here so that you can choose the closest. The greatest concentration is in suburban Kailua and Kaneohe. On the North Shore, the clapboard town of Haleiwa contains most of the area's markets. And along the Leeward Coast, Waianae is the central shopping area.

WINDWARD COAST GROCERY STORES

A convenient place to shop in Oahu's southeast corner is at the Koko Marina Shopping Center's **Foodland** in Hawaii Kai (7192 Kalanianaole Highway). Open 8:30 a.m. until 11 p.m. daily.

Proceeding north along the coast, there's **Mel's Market** (41-0129 Kalanianaole Highway), a small store in Waimanalo.

Then, in the suburban towns of Kailua and Kaneohe, you'll encounter large supermarkets. **Times Supermarket** (in Kailua Shopping Center on Kailua Road) is open from 8:30 a.m. to 10 p.m. Monday through Saturday, 8:30 a.m. to 9 p.m. Sunday. **Foodland** (Windward City Shopping Center at Kamehameha Highway and Kaneohe Bay Drive), in Kaneohe, is open from 8:30 a.m. to 11 p.m. daily.

These are good places to stock up, since the next large supermarket is the **IGA** way up in Hauula at the Hauula Kai Center on Kamehameha Highway (open 9 a.m. to 7 p.m. Monday through Thursday; 9 a.m. to 8 p.m. Friday and Saturday; and 9 a.m. to 4 p.m. on Sunday).

Between these major shopping complexes there are smaller facilities at **Kaawa Store** (41-484 Kamehameha Highway, Kaawa). North of Hauula, on Kamehameha Highway in Kahuku, there's a small **IGA**.

WINDWARD COAST HEALTH FOOD STORES

In the southeast corner of the island, there's **House of Nutrition** at the Koko Marina Shopping Center (7192 Kalanianaole Highway, Hawaii Kai). Further north, in Kailua, you might try **Kailua Health Food Center** (124 Oneawa Street), or in Kaneohe, **Living Foods** on Kamehameha Highway. Up near Oahu's northern tip, there's a **Better Life Health Food Store** (Laie Shopping Center; 55-510 Kamehameha Highway) in Laie. All these shops contain adequate supplies of natural food items.

WINDWARD COAST FRESH-FISH STORES

You can get fresh fish at **Masa and Joyce Fish Market** in the Temple Valley Shopping Center on the Kahekili Highway (Route 83), just north of Kaneohe.

Then, all along the Kamehameha Highway in Waiahole and Waikane valleys, there are small stands selling **fresh fruit**. The produce is grown right in this lush area and is sold pretty cheaply along the roadside.

NORTH SHORE GROCERY STORES

Haleiwa Supermarket (66-197 Kamehameha Highway, Haleiwa), the only large market on the entire north coast, is the best place to shop. There's also **Sunset Beach Store** (59-026 Kamehameha Highway), which has a small stock but is conveniently located near Sunset Beach.

NORTH SHORE HEALTH FOOD STORES

Celestial Natural Foods (Haleiwa Shopping Plaza, 66-197 Kamehameha Highway, Haleiwa) has an ample supply of health foods and fresh produce.

LEEWARD COAST GROCERY STORES

Big Way Supermarket (Waianae Mall Shopping Center, 86-120 Farrington Highway) in Waianae, is the prime spot in this area for shopping. It's a large supermarket open Monday through Friday from 9 a.m. to 8 p.m., with slightly shorter hours on the weekend.

LEEWARD COAST HEALTH FOOD STORES

Waianae Health Foods and Products (85-888 Farrington Highway) in Waianae has a modest stock of natural food items.

LEEWARD COAST FRESH-FISH STORES

If you're down near the southwest corner of Oahu, you might try **Toshi's Fish Market**, at 87-1784 Farrington Highway in Nanakuli, for an assortment of fresh island fish.

The Great Outdoors

Sightseeing

After visiting the historical spots around Honolulu, you'll probably be ready for a touch of the countryside. A circle island tour is the perfect counterpoint to the bustling lifestyle of the city. It will provide an opportunity to savor the time you've recently spent in Honolulu, while enjoying the luxurious scenery that the rest of Oahu has to offer.

If you trace the tour outlined in the following pages, you'll travel around the island in a counter-clockwise direction. It will carry you from Honolulu around Oahu's sandy southeast corner, up the Windward Coast, along the North Shore, back down through the Leilehua Plateau in the island's interior, and finally out west along the Leeward Coast.

WINDWARD COAST

DIAMOND HEAD TO MAKAPUU

Beginning from Honolulu's Waikiki district, follow Kalakaua Avenue to its terminus near the base of Diamond Head crater. From here you can explore east along Diamond Head Road and Kahala Avenue.This route passes **Diamond Head Lighthouse** and offers picturesque views of the south coast. It also travels past the posh **Kahala District**, featuring some of Honolulu's loveliest homes.

In Kahala, turn left on Kealaolu Avenue and follow it to Kalanianaole Highway (Route 72). This thoroughfare cuts through other residential areas, then climbs the slopes of 642-foot **Koko Head**, an extinct volcano. **Koko Crater**, the second hump on the horizon, rises to over 1,200 feet. This firepit, according to Hawaiian legend, is Pele's sister. It seems that Pele, goddess of volcanoes, was being pursued by a handsome demigod. Her sister, trying to distract the hot suitor from Pele, lay down seductively across the landscape and became a part of the bedrock.

From the top of Koko Head a side road and path lead down to **Hanauma Bay**. This breathtakingly beautiful bay is also an extinct volcano, one wall of which was breached by the sea. Today it's a marine preserve, filled with multicolored coral and teeming with underwater life.

The main road corkscrews along the coast, offering views of Lanai and Molokai, to an overlook at **Halona Blowhole**. Geysers of seawater blast through this lava tube, reaching dramatic heights when the ocean is turbulent.

Sandy Beach, one of Hawaii's finest bodysurfing spots, is just down the hill. Across from the beach a side road leads up to **Koko Crater Botanic Gardens** (next to Koko Head Stables), a 200-acre collection of cacti, plumeria, and other flowering plants.

The main road rounds Oahu's southeast corner and climbs to a scenic point above the windward shore. You can scan this stunning seascape for miles. That slope-faced islet just offshore is **Rabbit Island** and the distant headland is **Mokapu Peninsula**. The strand below the vista spot is **Makapuu Beach**. That complex of buildings is **Sea Life Park**, a titillating marine world which features "flying" dolphin shows and over 2,000 ocean species. (See the accompanying section for more details.)

MAKAPUU TO THE NORTH SHORE

The road descends along the shoreline and cuts between white-sand beaches and the **Koolau Range**. If wind and weather permit, you'll see hang gliders dusting the cliffs as they sail from the mountains down to the beach. That daggerpoint spire beyond Waimanalo is **Olomana Peak**, a favorite among equally daring rock climbers.

The highway continues to the suburban town of Kailua, where it intersects Route 61 (Kailua Road). If you go right a short distance along this second road you'll reach **Ulu Po Heiau** (it's behind the YMCA). The temple, according to legend, was constructed by Hobbit-like Menehunes who passed the building stones along a six-mile-long bucket brigade in a one-night construction project.

Back on Route 61 in the opposite direction you can pick up Route 83, which will carry you to **Kaneohe**. Past this bedroom community Route 83 is known as the Kamehameha Highway. Just outside town you can turn up Haiku Road to visit the graceful **Haiku Gardens** with an enchanting lily pond and acres of exotic plant life. Farther along Kamehameha Highway, don't bypass the **Valley of the Temples**. A truly inspiring sight here is the Buddhist **Byodo-In Temple** (nominal admission) shadowed by the sharply rising peaks of the Koolau Range.

The road runs along **Kaneohe Bay** and passes **Waiahole** and **Waikane Valleys**. This verdant area—which produces papayas, bananas, and sweet potatoes—has been a political battleground since the local government began evicting Hawaiian farmers. Those colorful roadside signs are protesting the bureaucracy's attempt to develop a prime agricultural region. Developers have already helped pollute Kaneohe Bay by destroying vegetation that protected against erosion. Today the bay, which has the only barrier reef in Hawaii, is clouded with silt.

TROPICAL THEME PARKS

Here you are on a dreamy island in the middle of the Pacific, over two thousand miles from the mainland United States. Sometimes it seems like historic old Honolulu is lulling you into the nineteenth century. But just when those sunny days and incandescent nights make you believe you're lost somewhere in time, the tropical environs present a feature to jolt you back to the here and now. Like Oahu's theme parks: what, after all, could be more modern than a theme park? And Oahu has several (all charge admission or other fees).

Right in Honolulu there's **Castle Park** (Salt Lake Boulevard, across from Aloha Stadium; 488-6822), an amusement park in the guise of a tropical kingdom. The castle, of course, is built on an island. There are also bumper boats, rope swings, and slippery slides, all located, naturally, in "Water Country."

Paradise Park (3737 Manoa Road; 988-2141), another Honolulu attraction, is set in fragrant Manoa Valley. King Kamehameha and his retinue once luxuriated in these fifteen acres of forest and gardens. Today the park has been developed into a maze of ponds, waterfalls, sinuous pathways, and lagoons. Brilliant flowers and plants grow thick as a rain forest throughout the grounds, and there's an aviary with trained birds. While wandering through the gardens, you can visit the historical gallery or take in a theatrical performance starring cockatoos and macaws.

Hawaii would have to have its own marine world: it's known as **Sea Life Park** (923-1531) and is situated outside Honolulu along the ocean at

Makapuu Point. Among the many features at this remarkable place is the Hawaiian Reef, a 300,000-gallon oceanarium inhabited by 2,000 sea creatures. To view the sharks, stingrays, and lesser species swimming about, you wind through a spiral viewing area that descends three fathoms along the tank's glass periphery. In the nearby Ocean Science Theatre, there are performances by trained dolphins, penguins, sea lions, and killer whales. The *Essex,* 70-foot replica of a whaling ship, lays anchored in the park's lagoon. And at the Pacific Whaling Museum (which, unlike the rest of the facilities, is free), Hawaii's harpoon history is traced further through displays of artifacts and scrimshaw artistry.

Foremost among Oahu's theme parks is the **Polynesian Cultural Center** (923-1861). Located along the Windward Coast in Laie, this 42-acre extravaganza recreates historic Polynesia. Meander about the grounds and you'll happen upon villages reminiscent of ancient Samoa, Tahiti, Fiji, Tonga, New Zealand, Hawaii, and the Marquesas. In the Tahitian village you can learn the vibrating *tamure* dance, in Samoa there will be exhibitions of a coconut shell game, in Tonga someone will pound mulberry bark into *tapa* cloth, while in Fiji exhibitors will beat out rhythms with bamboo poles. Connected by waterways, these recreated villages can be visited by canoe. There are also special events such as the "Pageant of the Long Canoes," a waterborne revue; and "Music Polynesia," a musical journey through South Pacific history. Operated by the Mormon Church, the Polynesian Cultural Center is one of Hawaii's major attractions. It provides an intriguing peek at the lifestyles of Pacific islanders, and is one theme park that should have a place on every visitor's itinerary.

Anchored just outside the bay is Mokolii Island, better known by its shape, **Chinaman's Hat**. Route 83 passes an **old sugar mill** and continues past a rock formation resembling a **Crouching Lion**. It rims coral-studded **Kahana Bay**, then, still crowding the coastline, traverses the tiny towns of **Punaluu** and **Hauula**. The aging **Hauula Door of Faith Church**, a tiny clapboard chapel, is surrounded by palms. Not far from here there's another old woodframe church, **Hauula Congregational Christian Church**, a wood-and-coral sanctuary dating to 1862.

In the nearby town of Laie you'll enter Mormon country. There's a temple here and a branch of Brigham Young University. This is also the site of the **Polynesian Cultural Center**, Hawaii's answer to Disneyland. (For a full description of this remarkable park, see the accompanying section.)

To experience a marvelous view of seascape and mountains, try the short side road which travels to Laie Point. There are two islets offshore, one of which has partially collapsed to create a natural arch. Then the main road goes past **Kahuku Sugar Mill**. In years past you could tour this old cane processing plant by trolley, a great way to learn what these factories were like in the days when sugar was king. Presently the mill is being renovated and is scheduled to open to the public at a future date.

NORTH SHORE

Broad beaches extend for miles along Oahu's turbulent north coast. **Sunset Beach** and **Waimea Bay**, two of the most famous surfing spots in the world, lie along this strip. Sunset is the site of the "Banzai Pipeline," where thunderous waves form into tube-shaped curls as they pass over a shallow reef. Waimea Bay sports the world's highest (up to thirty feet) surfable waves. Even if you're not a surfer, you might stop by to watch the incredible surfing performances here.

Between these two beaches, side roads lead to **Puu o Mahuka Heiau** and **Waimea Falls Park**. The *heiau*, Oahu's largest, is a split-level structure once used for human sacrifices. There's a fantastic view of the North Shore from this ethereal sanctuary. At Waimea Falls Park (638-8511), you can explore an 1,800-acre tropic preserve. The site of an old Hawaiian village, it's a supremely lush area filled with botanical gardens and archaeological ruins, and crisscrossed by hiking trails. This nature park also serves as a bird sanctuary. There's a visitor's center with restaurants and shops, plus a tram to carry you to the 55-foot falls for swimming and picnic outings. Admission charged.

Farther along Kamehameha Highway another side road, Kawailoa Drive, turns up through an **old plantation village**, where you'll see tin-roofed houses and a lovely old church. If you continue on the main road you'll arrive in **Haleiwa**, a former plantation town with a new facelift. Fortunately the architects who performed the operation had an eye to antiquity and designed modern shopping centers that blend comfortably into the village landscape. Most modern of all is the community: with its young surfer crowd Haleiwa has become a center of contemporary culture.

From here, head west and pick up Farrington Highway (Route 930). This country road parallels miles of unpopulated beachfront, and arrives at Dillingham Airfield, where you can take a **glider ride** along the Waianae Mountains (call 623-6711 for information). Beyond this landing strip, the road continues for several miles between ocean and mountains before turning into a very rugged dirt track. Though this unpaved portion might be passable in dry weather, the driving is generally so tortuous that I'd recommend hiking to **Kaena Point** on Oahu's northwest corner (see the "Hiking" section in this chapter).

ACROSS OAHU VIA THE LEILEHUA PLATEAU

Several highways lead from Haleiwa back to the Honolulu area. These cross the 1,000-foot **Leilehua** or **Schofield Plateau**, a rich agricultural area planted in pineapple and sugar. Stretching between the Koolau and Waianae Ranges, this tableland has become an important military headquarters. Schofield Barracks, Wheeler Air Force Base, and several other installations occupy huge stretches of land here. Wahiawa, a small, grimy city, is the region's commercial hub.

Somehow I've never found much in this part of Oahu. I usually pass quickly through this area on my way north or south. But there are a few places you might find worth touring.

For example, from Haleiwa south to Wahiawa you can take Route 82, a pretty road with excellent views of the Waianaes, or follow Route 80, which passes through verdant pineapple fields. If you take this latter highway, watch for a Hawaii Visitors Bureau sign pointing the way over a dirt road to **Kukaniloko**, a cluster of sacred birth stones marking the spot where Hawaiian royalty gave birth.

Route 82 connects with Route 99, which passes Schofield Barracks. If you have time for a scenic detour, pull up to the sentry gate at Schofield and ask directions to **Kolekole Pass**. It was through this notch that Japanese planes streaked toward Pearl Harbor. You'll be directed through Schofield up into the Waianaes. When you reach Kolekole Pass, there's another sentry gate. Ask the guard to let you continue a short distance farther to the observation point. From here the Waianaes fall away precipitously to a plain which rolls gently to the sea. There's an astonishing view of Oahu's west coast. If you're denied permission to pass the sentry point, then take the footpath which begins just before the gate, leading up the hill. From near the cross at the top, you'll have a partial view of both the Waianaes' western face and the central plateau region.

From the Wahiawa-Schofield area south toward Honolulu, you can barrel down either the H-2 superhighway or Route 99, or take the slower, more scenic Route 750. This last road, which parallels the Waianaes and offers marvelous views, is my favorite.

LEEWARD COAST

From Honolulu you can visit Oahu's dry, sunny western shore by traveling west on Route H-1 or Route 90. If you want to tour a prime sugar-growing area, take Route 90 past Pearl Harbor, then turn left on Fort Weaver Road (Route 76). This country lane leads to the plantation town of **Ewa**. With its busy sugar mill and trim houses, Ewa is an enchanting throwback to the days when sugar was king. It's a terrific town to just wander around.

Near Oahu's southwest corner, Routes H-1 and 90 converge to become the Farrington Highway (Route 93). This road heads up the west coast through the tableland which separates the **Waianae Range** and the ocean. It's a region of stark beauty, resembling the Southwest, with rocky crags and cactus-studded hills.

Hawaiian and Samoan farmers populate the Waianae coast. The **Waianae Hawaiian Heritage Cultural Cen-**

ter (85-067 Farrington Highway) gives classes in various Hawaiian arts such as hula, quilting, or plaiting arts. Call the Center (696-6611) if you're interested in mastering one of these skills. If you turn up Mailiilii Street in Waianae, you'll pass placid Hawaiian homesteads and farmlands. This side road also provides sweeping views of the mountains.

The highway continues along the coast past several beaches and parks. Across from Kaena Point State Park you'll come upon **Moi Hole**, a lava cavern large enough for exploring. And beyond that, where the road turns to dirt, lies **Yokohama Bay**, with its curving sand beach. **Kaena Point Satellite Tracking Station** sits atop the nearby mountains. The road past Yokohama is partially passable by auto, but, it's very rough. If you want to explore **Kaena Point** from this side of the island, I recommend hiking. It's about two miles to the northwest corner of Oahu, past tidepools teeming with marine life.

Beaches and Parks

Oahu might be Hawaii's most populous isle, but it certainly does not lack for remote realms and secluded beaches. There are also excellent state and county parks on the Capital Island, with facilities for overnighters and daytrippers alike. So when the spirit motivates you, head for the country and see if you can't uncover a private piece of paradise.

WINDWARD COAST BEACHES AND PARKS

Hanauma Bay Beach Park—One of Oahu's prettiest and most popular beaches, this curving swath of white sand extends for almost a half-mile. The botton of the bay is a maze of coral reef, and the entire area has been designated a marine preserve. As a result, the skin diving is unmatched and the fish are tame enough to eat from your hand.

You can also hike along rock ledges fringing the bay and explore some mind-boggling tidepools. Crowded though it is, this is one strand that should not be bypassed.

Facilities: Picnic area, restrooms, showers, snack bar, volleyball court, snorkeling equipment rentals, and lifeguards. One mile to restaurants and markets at Koko Marina Shopping Center.

Camping: None.

Swimming: Very good.

Snorkeling: Superb. But beware of Witches Brew, a turbulent area on the bay's right side, and the Molokai Express, a wicked current sweeping across the mouth of the bay. No fish spearing.

Surfing: None.

Fishing: Strictly prohibited.

Getting there: Located about nine miles east of Waikiki. Take Route 72 to Koko Head, then turn onto the side road near the top of the promontory. This leads to a parking lot; leave your vehicle and walk the several hundred yards down the path to the beach.

Sandy Beach—This long, wide beach is a favorite among Oahu's youth. The shorebreak makes it one of the finest, and most dangerous, bodysurfing beaches in the islands. It's a pleasant place to sunbathe, but if you go swimming, plan to negotiate a pounding shoreline. Should you want to avoid the crowds, head over to **Wamamalu Beach** next door to the east.

Facilities: Picnic area, restrooms, showers. Three miles to the restaurants and markets in Koko Marina Shopping Center.

Camping: Not permitted.

Swimming: Mediocre.

Snorkeling: Poor.

Surfing: Good, and very popular. Beware of rip currents.

Fishing: Among the principal catches are *ulua, papio*, and *mamao*.

Getting there: Head out Route 72 (Kalanianaole Highway) about twelve miles east of Waikiki.

Makapuu Beach Park—It's set in a very pretty spot with lava cliffs in the background and Rabbit Island just offshore. This is a short, wide rectangle of white sand favored by Hawaii's bodysurfers. With no protecting reef and a precipitous shoreline, Makapuu is inundated by awesome swells that send wave riders crashing onto shore. Necks and backs are broken with frightening regularity here, so if the waves are large and you're inexperienced—play the spectator. If you take the plunge, prepare for a battering!

Facilities: Picnic area, restrooms, lifeguard. There's a restaurant across the road in **Sea Life Park.**

Camping: Not permitted.

Swimming: Though okay in summer, at other times the ocean is too rough. This is Hawaii's most famous bodysurfing beach.

Snorkeling: Usually poor.

Surfing: Not permitted.

Fishing: Looks good for *ulua, papio,* and *mamao.*

Getting there: Located on Route 72 (Kalanianaole Highway) about thirteen miles east of Waikiki.

Waimanalo Beach Park—Located at the southeast end of Waimanalo's three-and-a-half-mile-long beach, this is a spacious 38-acre park. It's studded with ironwood trees and equipped with numerous recreation facilities.

Both this county park and **Waimanalo Bay State Recreation Area,** a mile farther north, are excellent spots for picnicking, swimming, and sunbathing. The state park is farther removed from the highway in a grove of ironwood trees known to local residents as "Sherwood Forest," but camping is permitted only at the county facility.

Facilities: Picnic area, restrooms, showers, playground, basketball court, baseball field at Waimanalo Beach Park. Restaurants and markets nearby.

Camping: Tent and trailer. County permit required.

Swimming: Good; well-protected. State park has good bodysurfing.

Snorkeling: Good.

Surfing: Poor.

Fishing: The most frequently caught fish here is *papio;* bonefish, milkfish, and goatfish are also common.

Getting there: Located at 41-471 Kalanianaole Highway (Route 72) about fifteen miles east of Waikiki.

Bellows Beach Park—This is one of Oahu's most luxurious parks. There's a broad white-sand beach bordered by ironwood trees, with a marvelous view of the Koolau mountains. The catch is that Bellows Park is situated on a military base and is open to visitors only from Friday noon until 8 a.m. Monday.

Facilities: Picnic area, showers, restroom, lifeguard. Restaurants and markets are about a mile away in Waimanalo.

Camping: County permit required.

Swimming: Very good.

Snorkeling: Good.

Surfing: Good for beginners.

Fishing: The most abundant species at Bellows is *papio,* followed by bonefish, milkfish, and goatfish.

Getting there: Turn off Kalanianaole Highway (Route 72) toward Bellows Air Force Station. The park is located near Waimanalo, about seventeen miles east of Waikiki.

Malaekahana State Recreation Area and **Goat Island**—This is a rare combination. The Malaekahana facility is one of the island's prettiest parks. It's a tropical wonderland filled with palm, *hala*, and ironwood trees, graced with a curving white-sand beach.

And there's Goat Island, just off shore. Simply put, if you visit Oahu and don't explore it, you'll be missing an extraordinary experience. It's a small, low-lying island covered with scrub growth and scattered ironwood trees. On the windward side is a coral beach; to leeward lies a crescent-shaped white-sand beach that seems drawn from a South Seas dream. Goat Island (which no longer contains goats) is now a state bird refuge, so you might see wedge-tailed shearwaters nesting. You can camp, picnic, swim, do anything here, as long as you don't disturb the birds. Goat Island will return the favor—there'll be nothing here to disturb you either.

Facilities: Showers, bathrooms, barbeque pits.

Camping: State permit required.

Swimming: Good; the leeward beach is shallow and well-protected.

Snorkeling: Good.

Surfing: Long paddle out to winter breaks with left slide.

Fishing: You may well reel in *papio*, the most abundant fish along here; goatfish, milkfish, and bonefish are also caught.

Getting there: Located on Kamehameha Highway (Route 83) in Laie about twenty-three miles north of Kaneohe.

Hawaii Nudist Park—Hawaii's only nudist colony is a 247-acre park near Oahu's northern tip. Privacy is the password to this beachfront retreat: the park is quite secluded and protected against intruders. The beach is sandy but the ocean bottom is coral, which makes for great sunbathing but hinders swimming. The big drawback is the admission price: $20 a day ($41 a week) for a single person or couple. But if you like to sunbathe in the buff, and enjoy the company of fellow nudists, you might check it out.

Facilities: Picnic area, restrooms, showers, recreation center, playground, and snack bar. There are also one-room cabins to rent for $20 a night. These are well-maintained shacks with stoves, refrigerators, gas lamps, and community bathrooms.

Camping: Camping privileges are included in the daily admission fee.

Swimming: Fair.

Snorkeling: Good.

Fishing: Watch for *papio*, but milkfish, bonefish, and goatfish may turn up too.

Getting there: The park's exact location is confidential. For directions and further information contact Hawaii Nudist Park, P.O. Box 8417, Honolulu, Oahu, HI 96815 (949-3363).

NORTH SHORE BEACHES AND PARKS

Sunset Beach—If you've ever owned a surfboard, or even a Beach Boys album, you know this beach. Sunset is synonymous with surfing: it's one of the most famous, challenging, and dangerous surf spots in the world. During winter months, fifteen- and twenty-foot waves are common.

The beach, two miles long and about two hundred feet wide, is one of Oahu's largest. I think the best way to do Sunset is by starting from Ehukai Beach Park. From here you can go left to the "Banzai Pipeline," where crushing waves build along a shallow coral reef to create tube-like formations. To the right lies "Sunset," with equally spectacular surfing waves.

Facilities: Ehukai Beach Park has picnic areas, restrooms, and showers. Nearby there are also markets and restaurants.

Camping: Not permitted.

Swimming: Fair in summer; extremely dangerous in winter. The same conditions that make for great surfing also create powerful rip currents and longshore currents. People die here. Be very careful, particularly from September to April.

Snorkeling: Poor.

Surfing: See above.

Fishing: The most frequent catches are *papio, menpachi*, and *ulua*.

Getting there: Ehukai Beach Park is off Kamehameha Highway (Route 83) about seven miles northeast of Haleiwa.

Waimea Bay Beach Park—If Sunset is *one* of the most famous surfing spots in the world, Waimea is *the* most famous. The biggest surfable waves in the world roll into this pretty blue bay.

There's a wide white-sand beach and a pleasant park with a tree-studded lawn. It's a marvelous place for picnicking and sunbathing. In summer you can swim, and in winter you can sunbathe and watch the surfers.

Facilities: Picnic area, restrooms, showers, lifeguard. Restaurant and market about a mile away near Sunset Beach.

Camping: Not permitted.

Swimming: Good in summer; extremely dangerous in winter. Good bodysurfing in shorebreak.

Snorkeling: Good when the bay is calm.

Surfing: See above.

Fishing: The common game fish caught here are *papio, menpachi*, and *ulua*.

Getting there: On Kamehameha Highway (Route 83) about five miles northeast of Haleiwa.

LEEWARD COAST BEACHES AND PARKS

Keaiwa Heiau State Recreation Area—Amazing as it sounds, this is a wooded retreat within easy driving distance of Honolulu. Situated in the Koolau foothills overlooking Pearl

Harbor, it contains a *heiau* once used by Hawaiian healers. There's an arboretum of medicinal plants, a forest extending to the far reaches of the mountains, and a network of hiking trails.

Facilities: Picnic area and restrooms. Markets and restaurants several miles away.

Camping: Tents only. State permit required.

Getting there: Located in Aiea Heights. To get there from Honolulu, take Route 90 west to Aiea, then follow Aiea Heights Drive to the park.

Makaha Beach Park—Some of the finest surfing in the world takes place right offshore here. This is the home of the Makaha International Surfing Championship, which attracts expert surfers every year.

For more relaxed sports, there's a white-sand beach to sunbathe on and some good places to skin dive. The precipitous Waianae Mountains loom behind the park.

Facilities: Picnic tables, restrooms, showers. A market and restaurants are nearby.

Camping: Not permitted.

Swimming and Snorkeling: Both are good when the sea is calm; otherwise, exercise extreme caution.

Surfing: Terrific; see above.

Fishing: Primary game fish caught here are *papio, ulua, moano,* and *menpachi.*

Getting there: Located on Farrington Highway (Route 93) in Makaha, two miles north of Waianae.

Yokohama Bay—This curving stretch of white sand is the last beach along Oahu's northwest coast. With the Waianae Range in the background and coral reefs offshore, it's a particularly lovely spot. Though officially a state park, the area is largely undeveloped. You can walk from Yokohama past miles of tidepools to Oahu's northwest corner at Kaena Point. Yokohama Bay is a prime region for beach lovers and explorers both.

Facilities: Restrooms.

Camping: Not permitted.

Swimming: Good when the sea is calm, but exercise extreme caution if the surf is up.

Snorkeling: Excellent if the sea is calm.

Surfing: Summer breaks up to fifteen feet over a shallow reef; left slide.

Fishing: Principal game fish caught in this area are *papio, ulua, moano,* and *menpachi.*

Getting there: Located at the end of the paved section of Farrington Highway (Route 93), about nine miles north of Waianae.

Hiking

Oahu is laced with hiking trails. Whatever challenge you seek will probably be found right here. You can stroll along a rocky shoreline, climb a volcano, trek into the mountains, or backpack through a rain forest.

WINDWARD COAST TRAILS

There are several excellent hikes along this raindrenched shore. The first few are within ten miles of Waikiki, near **Hanauma Bay.** From the beach at Hanauma you can hike two miles along the coast and cliffs to the Halona Blowhole. This trek passes Toilet Bowl, a unique tidepool with a hole in the bottom which causes it to fill and then flush with the wave action. Waves sometimes wash the rocks along this path, so be prepared to get wet.

At the intersection where the short road leading down toward Hanauma Bay branches from Kalanianaole Highway (Route 72), there are two other trails. **Koko Head Trail**, a one-mile hike to the top of a volcanic cone, starts on the ocean side of the highway. This trek features some startling views of Hanauma Bay, Diamond Head, and the Koolau Mountains. Another one-mile hike, along **Koko Crater Trail,** leads from the highway up to a 1,208-foot peak. The views from this crow's nest are equally spectacular.

There are several other particularly pretty hikes much farther north, near the village of Hauula. **Sacred Falls Trail** (2.2 miles) gently ascends into a canyon and arrives at a waterfall and swimming hole. The trailhead for this popular trek is near Kamehameha Highway (Route 83) just south of Hauula.

Then, in Hauula, if you turn off Kamehameha Highway and head inland about a quarter-mile up Hauula Homestead Road, you'll come to Maakua Road. Walk up Maakua Road,

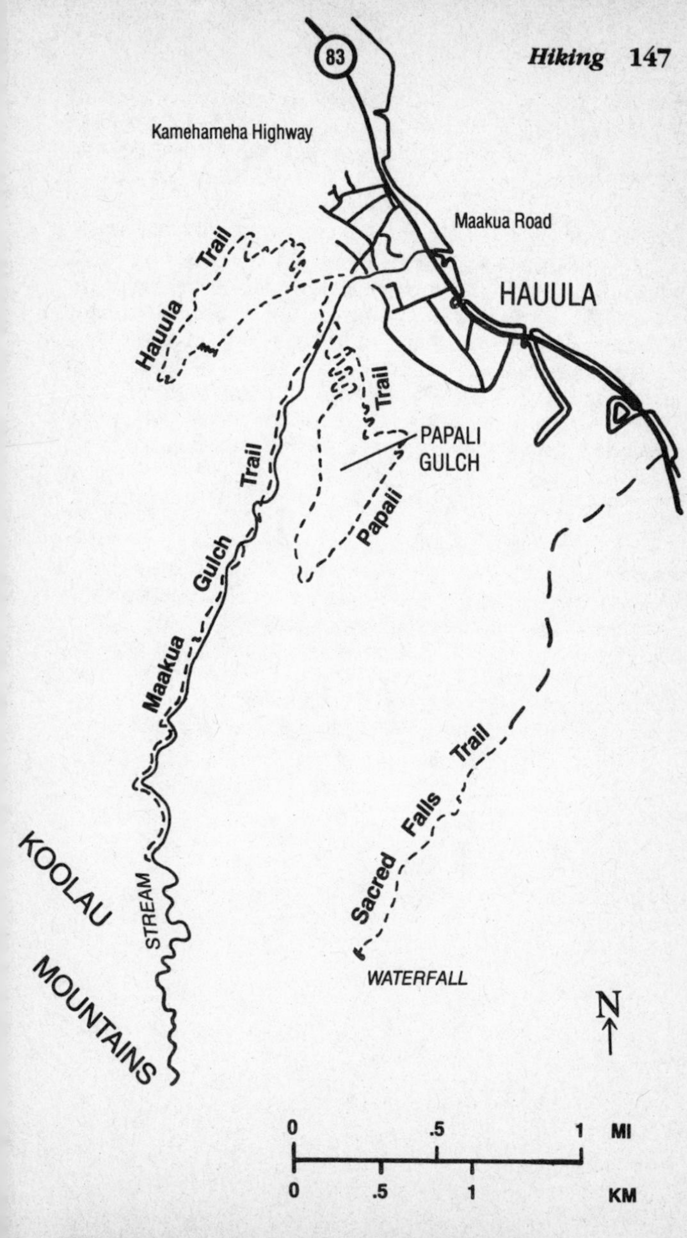
83
Kamehameha Highway
Maakua Road
HAUULA
Hauula Trail
Trail
PAPALI GULCH
Papali
Maakua Gulch Trail
KOOLAU MOUNTAINS
STREAM
Sacred Falls Trail
WATERFALL
N
0 .5 1 MI
0 .5 1 KM
WINDWARD COAST TRAILS

which leads into the woods. About 300 yards after entering the woods, the road forks. **Maakua Gulch Trail** branches to the left. If you continue straight ahead you'll be on **Hauula Trail**, but if you veer left onto Maakua Gulch Trail, you'll encounter another trail branching to the left in about 150 yards. This is **Papali Trail** (also known as Maakua Trail).

Maakua Gulch Trail (3 miles), en route to a small waterfall, traverses a rugged canyon with extremely steep walls. Part of the trail lies along the stream bed, so be ready to get wet. **Hauula Trail** (2.5 miles) ascends along two ridges and provides fine vistas of the Koolau Mountains and the Windward Coast. **Papali Trail** (2.5 miles) drops into Papali Gulch, then climbs high along a ridge from which you can view the surrounding countryside.

NORTH SHORE AND LEEWARD COAST TRAILS

You can approach the trail to **Kaena Point** either from the north or the west shoreline. It's a dry, rock-strewn path which leads to Oahu's northwest tip. There are tidepools and swimming spots en route, plus spectacular views of a rugged, uninhabited coastline. To get to the trailhead just drive to the end of the paved portion of Route 930 on the north shore or Route 93 on the west coast. Then follow the jeep trail out to Kaena Point. Either way, it's about a two-mile trek.

Addresses and Phone Numbers

OAHU ISLAND

Bus Schedule—(531-1611)
Coast Guard (search and rescue emergencies)—(536-4336)
Surf Report—(836-1952)
Taxi—Charley's Taxi (531-1333); Sida Taxi (836-0011)
Weather Report—(836-0121)
(For complete Honolulu listings, see the end of Chapter III.)

WINDWARD COAST

Ambulance—(911)

Fire Department—(911)

Laundromat—Kailua Laundromat, Aulike Street, Kailua (261-9201)

Police Department—(911)

NORTH SHORE

Ambulance—(911)
Fire Department—(911)
Police Department—(911)

LEEWARD COAST

Ambulance—(911)
Fire Department—(911)
Laundromat—Waianae Self-Service Laundry, Waianae Mall Shopping Center, 86-120 Farrington Highway (696-9108)
Police Department—(911)

CHAPTER VI

The Neighbor Islands

Where to Go

Deciding to take a vacation in Honolulu is easy, and touring the rest of the island of Oahu is sheer joy. The hard part comes if you decide to visit the Neighbor Islands. All five are remarkably beautiful places, each with unique features to offer the traveler. You'll be confronted with a decision tantamount to choosing between Shangri-La and the Garden of Eden.

To help you decide, I'll briefly describe the key features of each. Eventually it's nice to tour them all, but during a single Honolulu sojourn you'll probably want to venture out to only one or two.

My personal favorites are the Big Island and Kauai, and I often recommend to friends unfamiliar with Hawaii that they visit these two islands. That way they manage to travel both ends of the chain, experiencing the youngest and most rugged, and the oldest and most lush, of all the islands. The two offer a startling contrast, one that quickly shatters any illusion that all the islands are alike.

The island of **Hawaii**, or the **Big Island**, is true to its nickname. Located at the southeastern end of the Hawaiian chain, and dominated by two 13,000-foot volcanoes, this giant measures over twice the size of all the other islands combined. It's a great place to mountain climb and explore live volcanoes, to swim along the sun-splashed Kona Coast, or to tour orchid farms in the verdant city of Hilo.

Maui, the second largest island, is rapidly becoming Hawaii's favorite destination for young visitors. Haleakala alone, the extraordinary crater which dominates the island, makes the Valley Isle worth touring. The island also sports many of Hawaii's prettiest beaches and provides an offshore breeding ground for rare humpback whales.

Directly to the west, lying in Maui's wind-shadow, sits the smallest and most secluded island. **Lanai** is an explorer's paradise, with a network of jeep trails leading to hidden beaches and scenic mountain ridges. There are only 2,000 people and about twenty miles of paved road here. If you're seeking an idyllic retreat, this is the place.

Molokai, slightly larger but nearly as remote, provides another extraordinary hideaway. With white-sand beaches, a mountainous interior, and a large population of Hawaiians, the Friendly Isle retains a unique sense of old Hawaii. Here you can visit a leper colony on the windswept Kalaupapa Peninsula, a pilgrimage that could prove to be the most awesome of all your experiences in Hawaii.

Hawaii's prettiest, most luxuriant island lies at the northwestern end of the chain. **Kauai**, with its jewel-like beaches and uninhabited valleys, is a place you shouldn't miss. Along the north shore are misty cliffs that fall precipitously to the sea; from the island's center rises a mountain that receives more rainfall than any place on earth; and along Kauai's southern flank there's a startling desert region reminiscent of the Southwest. With its wildly varied climates and terrain, this island is like a small continent.

How to Go

Once you've chosen a destination, you'll find there are no commercial boats plying the waters between Honolulu and the Neighbor Islands. The only transportation is by plane.

Aloha Airlines and **Hawaiian Air**, the state's major carriers, provide frequent inter-island jet service. If you're looking for smooth, rapid, comfortable service, this is certainly it. You'll be buckled into your seat, offered a low-cost cocktail, and whisked to your destination within about twenty minutes.

Also, if you have a round-trip ticket from the mainland United States on a major airline, you'll qualify for the "joint fare," which permits you to island hop all over Hawaii, paying a single standard fee for each island you visit. These airlines also offer other budget fares, which change frequently in price and restrictions. So it's best to check with your travel agent for the best current deal. You might also consider flying via **Mid-Pacific Air**, Hawaii's newest inter-island carrier.

Another way to save money is by joining either Aloha Airlines or Hawaiian Air's travel clubs. After paying a $5 membership fee, you're entitled to twenty-five percent off the regular fare on any flight scheduled before 8 a.m. or after 3 p.m. If you travel before 6:30 a.m. or after 6:30 p.m., you'll save fifty percent. Regardless of which program you select, it will cost extra to ship a bike.

Now that you know how to fly quickly and comfortably, let me tell you about the most exciting way to get between islands. Several small airlines—**Royal Hawaiian Air Service, Air Hawaii, Air Molokai, Princeville Airways**, and others—fly twin-engine propeller planes. These small, eight-passenger airplanes travel at low altitudes and moderate speeds over the islands. Next to chartering a helicopter, this is the finest way to see Hawaii from the air.

The service is very personalized; often the pilot will point out landmarks along the route, and sometimes even fly out of the way to show you points of particular interest. I always fly on Royal Hawaiian Air Service when I'm in the islands; I highly recommend the company.

I once flew from Honolulu to Kona on Royal Hawaiian. So that I'd get a better view, the captain suggested that I sit up front in the co-pilot's seat. After taking off in a wide arc around Honolulu, we passed close enough to Diamond Head to gaze down into the crater, then headed across the Kaiwi Channel to Molokai. Since we had to pick up passengers at Molokai's lonely airstrip, the pilot gave me a tour of the island. We paralleled the island's rugged north face, where sharp cliffs laced with waterfalls drop thousands of feet to the sea. Then we swept in toward Maui for a view of Haleakala Crater, and continued past the Big Island's snowtipped volcanoes before touching down in Kona. All for the price of an airline ticket!

Rates for Royal Hawaiian Air Service and the other companies are very competitive when compared with the inter-island jets. Coupled with the fact that your ticket on the smaller carriers is worth a guided tour, you really can't do better than booking your flights on these sturdy propeller planes.

Index

Recommended Reading

Hawaii, by James Michener. Bantam Books, 1978. This lengthy historic novel skillfully blends fact and fiction, dramatically tracing the entire course of Hawaiian history.

Hawaii Pono, by Lawrence H. Fuchs. Harcourt Brace Jovanovich, 1961. A brilliant sociological study of twentieth-century Hawaii which vividly portrays the island's ethnic groups.

Hawaii: The Sugar-Coated Fortress, by Francine Du Plessix Gray. Random House, 1972. A hard-hitting analysis of modern-day Hawaii which details the tragic effect Western civilization has had on the Hawaiian people.

Hawaiian Antiquities, by David Malo. Bishop Museum Press, 1971. Written by a Hawaiian scholar in the nineteenth century, this study contains a wealth of information on pre-European Hawaiian culture.

Hawaiian Hiking Trails, by Craig Chisholm. Touchstone Press, 1975. The best single-volume hiking guide available, this handbook provides excellent descriptions of Hawaii's most popular treks.

Hidden Hawaii: The Adventurer's Guide, by Ray Riegert. And/Or Press, 1979, 1982. A companion volume to *Hidden Honolulu,* this guide explores all the Hawaiian islands.

The Legends and Myths of Hawaii, by David Kalakaua. Charles E. Tuttle Company, 1972. Written by Hawaii's last king, this fascinating collection includes fables of the great chiefs and priests who once ruled the islands.

Polynesian Researches: Hawaii, by William Ellis. Charles E. Tuttle Company, 1969. This missionary's journal originally appeared in the 1820s. Despite some tedious sermonizing, it poignantly portrays Hawaii at a historic crossroads and graphically describes volcanoes and other natural phenomena on the Big Island.

Shoal of Time, by Gavan Daws. University of Hawaii, 1974. The finest history written on Hawaii, this volume is not only informative but entertaining as well.

About the Author

Leslie Henriques

Hidden Honolulu is another in a series of travel books by Ray Riegert. A companion volume, *Hidden Hawaii*, has become a top-seller since its release several years ago. Similar guides, exploring "Hidden" realms all over the world, are also in the planning stage.

In addition to authoring these handy guides, Ray Riegert is a frequent contributor to newspapers, magazines, and broadcast media throughout the United States and Canada. He has written for "Travel & Leisure," Gannett News Service, "Diversion," Pacific News Service, Pacifica radio network, and numerous other media. Ray has even helped bury a few publications with his prose, having worked on assignments for "New Times," "Seven Days," and the dearly departed "Berkeley Barb."

He and his wife, travel photographer Leslie Henriques, live in the San Francisco Bay Area. Ray's special interest is the Pacific. As a longstanding member of the Pacific Area Travel Association, he has written extensively on the emerging culture and current concerns of the Pacific Rim.

A Note from the Author

An alert, adventurous reader is as important as a travel writer in keeping a guidebook up-to-date and accurate. So if you happen upon a great restaurant, discover a hidden locale, or (heaven forbid) find an error in the text, I'd appreciate hearing from you. Just write to:

Ray Riegert
And/Or Press
P.O Box 2246
Berkeley, CA 94702